THE COLOR OF LOVE
UNDERSTANDING GOD'S ANSWER
TO RACISM, SEPARATION AND DIVISION

by

Creflo A. Dollar Jr.

HARRISON HOUSE
Tulsa, Oklahoma

The Color of Love
Understanding God's Answer to Racism, Separation and Division
ISBN 1-57794-024-5
Copyright © 1997 by Creflo A. Dollar Jr.
World Changers Ministries Christian Center
P. O. Box 490124
College Park, Georgia 30349

Published by Harrison House, Inc.
P. O. Box 35035
Tulsa, Oklahoma 74153

CONTENTS

INTRODUCTION

The Lord has given me a hard task. He has put it on my heart to deal with the spirit of division, separation and racism at work within the Body of Christ.

I see racism, particularly, as just another attempt of the devil to stop what God wants done in the Church. This is a subject the Church has not wanted to deal with; but if we don't start dealing with it, it will destroy our lives.

In this study, I will show you the solution to racism. I will show you what we in the Body of Christ have to do so that we all can come together.

Have you wondered, *Where is God's power in the Church?* Maybe it is being blocked by the sin that we have kept covered up, because nobody has wanted to deal with it. Why can't we all come together as brothers and sisters in Christ? When we do, we will begin walking in an anointing like never before in our lives.

God is calling all of His people — brothers and sisters in Christ from different racial backgrounds — to begin growing in love with one another. We must become one. When we do, the devil won't be able to stay among us, because the power of God will come over us like we have never experienced.

My attempt in this study is not to convert every person in the world so that they will receive everything I have to say about this subject. My objective is to make sure that if division is in the Church — and it is — we get rid of it. For too long, we have not spoken from our pulpits about this division. We have not really dealt with it among our churches. But now we must!

Using my church in College Park, Georgia, as a testing ground, I have dropped little bombs from the pulpit, then checked the reactions of the people. To keep a balance in my teachings, I have spent time sitting and talking about the subjects with other members of the Body of Christ.

In this book, I will not be giving you just my opinion; I will be taking you on an adventure through the Word of God. There are lots of drug pushers at work in the world, but I am a Word pusher. I want to get you high on God's Word. I would never step away from the Word when trying to handle a subject such as this, and this topic *must* be handled spiritually.

The first time I ministered this message was at a national conference of pastors. But before I could really cover it in depth, I felt it was important to share on the subjects of faith and covenant. That's what I will be doing in this book.

When God first began dealing with me about ministering on the problems of division, separation and racism within the Body of Christ, I said, "Oh God, not me." I wanted to avoid it at all cost. I said, "No, Lord, I'm not going to deal with it. Let somebody else do it and mess up his ministry. Not me, please!"

Then our office received a letter from a sixty-five-year-old black woman, whose comments went something like this:

> I was upset and angry at you concerning the reconciling between blacks and whites. You are just saying these things to

please those white folks. You don't understand how it has really been. They wouldn't let me eat in their restaurants or drink out of their water fountains.

This woman accused me of having lost my identity as a black person, then she closed her letter by saying:

> Yes, I am a bitter, black woman, but I can't help it — or I don't want to help it. I will *never* forgive!

Her letter gave me the confirmation I needed to preach this message to the Body of Christ. I realized, then, the need to face this problem head-on.

When I heard we had received this letter in our office, I asked for a copy of it. I wanted to keep it as a reminder of the strong deception the devil has put over on God's people. Every time I feel I want to quit dealing with this subject of racism, I can pull out that letter and read it again. It reminds me of how important and vital this message is to all of us in the Body of Christ.

I am so glad God isn't sitting there on His throne with the same kind of attitude towards mankind that that lady expressed to me in her letter. But what if God felt that way?

He could be looking at us and saying:

"Look what those people did against Me all those years. They wouldn't keep My Word. They wouldn't pray to Me. Then they tortured and killed My Son. They flogged Him with a cat-o'-nine-tails, made Him drag a cross through the streets, then nailed Him to that cross where He hung until He died. And now they are asking Me to have mercy on them. It makes Me repent that I ever made them in the first place!"

Now don't think God wasn't tempted to destroy mankind. After the first man, Adam, messed up in the Garden, things just went downhill from there. By the time Noah entered the picture, God was ready to close the book on that human experiment. But the force of reconciliation came into play. God's grace protected Noah and his family when the rest of mankind was destroyed by the Flood. (Genesis ch. 2, 3, 6.)

It makes no difference how bad your life is now, or has ever been. The fact is, you cannot keep looking at a white man or a black man and hold him responsible for your hatred or bondage in the past. Feeling that way will only keep you in strife now, and your bondage will become even greater, for it will be eternal.

No matter how miserable the situation in your life may have been, it isn't worth missing out on heaven because you feel animosity or hatred towards people whose skin is another color.

In Matthew 5:44 Jesus said:

But I say unto you, Love your enemies, bless them that curse you, do good to them that hate you, and pray for them which despitefully use you, and persecute you.

As Christian people, when Jesus said, **Love your enemies,** He meant all of them — our black enemies and our white enemies, too.

When He said, **Do good to them that hate you,** He didn't say you were to do good to everybody — except for *that* white man or *that* black man. You are walking in strong deception if you think you can call yourself a Christian, whether white or black, and still feel hatred towards that brother or sister whom you see every day.

Let's face it: we, as true believers in Jesus Christ, have a great task ahead of us.

People will come to me and say: "But you don't understand. I have a right to hate those people over there. I have a right to hold things against them after what they did."

My response to them would be based on Matthew 6:15, where

Jesus said: **If ye forgive not men their trespasses, neither will your Father forgive your trespasses.** I would say to them: "If you are a child of God and you don't forgive others, neither can your heavenly Father forgive you."

As a result of taking this step publicly, I may be called every name that can be imagined, but I have been given a charge from God, and I must keep it. Just as He did for everyone else who will receive Him, God gave His Son that my almost-gone-to-hell soul could be saved, that I might serve Him in this present age. I have been called to do my Master's will, and this calling must be fulfilled to glorify Almighty God.

But, you know, this isn't limited to Pastor Creflo A. Dollar Jr. All of us in the Body of Christ have been given the ministry of reconciliation. It is time that we reconcile with one another, because something much greater is at stake here: the outpouring of the anointing of Almighty God.

By taking steps to reconcile for the past, we in the Body of Christ will experience one of the most powerful revivals of reconciliation we have ever seen. When this reconciliation takes place, there will be an increase of the anointing that cannot be denied.

Once the world starts seeing the Church reconciling, they will take note of the example and realize they can do it, too.

I am ready for the challenge. How about you?

CHAPTER 1

THE SPIRIT OF DIVISION

Jesus said a house divided against itself will not stand and Satan divided against Satan cannot stand. (Mark 3:25,26.) So, Satan is doing his very best to divide and conquer the Body of Christ by using the spirit of strife and the spirit of confusion, which are associated with the spirit of division.

All of this is designed to stop our increase in the Church of Jesus Christ. If we keep falling into the same traps that have separated us throughout all of history, we will continue allowing the devil to beat our brains in.

I want to begin by looking at Matthew, chapter 24. I believe it will shed some light on things happening in the world today. We Christians have probably read this chapter over and over again when dealing with the end time and the end of the world. We believe without a doubt that this world is coming to an end. We recognize that science is finally catching up with the Word of God.

On one TV talk show, people were proving that, without a shadow of a doubt, prayer works. They actually had scientific evidence. They were a little confused in other areas, but I was rejoicing that they were trying to convince people that prayer works. Now as soon as they realize that it is Almighty God Who should be receiving their prayers, they will be headed in the right direction.

I'm telling you right now, if you are praying to Buddha or Mohammed or the Reverend Moon, you are wasting your time. They will never be able to answer your prayers. *You will have to go higher than the Moon in order to get to the Son!*

Let's read this entire passage of Scripture from Matthew, chapter 24. Jesus is talking here about things believers need to know so that they will not be deceived.

> *And Jesus went out, and departed from the temple: and his disciples came to him for to shew him the buildings of the temple.*
>
> *And Jesus said unto them, See ye not all these things? verily I say unto you, There shall not be left here one stone upon another, that shall not be thrown down.*
>
> *And as he sat upon the mount of Olives, the disciples came unto him privately, saying, Tell us, when shall these things be? and what shall be the sign of thy coming, and of the end of the world?*
>
> *And Jesus answered and said unto them, Take heed that no man deceive you.*
>
> *For many shall come in my name, saying, I am Christ; and shall deceive many.*
>
> *And ye shall hear of wars and rumours of wars: see that ye be not troubled: for all these things must come to pass, but the end is not yet.*
>
> *For nation shall rise against nation, and kingdom against kingdom: and there shall be famines, and pestilences, and earthquakes, in divers places.*
>
> *All these are the beginning of sorrows.*

Then shall they deliver you up to be afflicted, and shall kill you: and ye shall be hated of all nations for my name's sake.

And then shall many be offended, and shall betray one another, and shall hate one another.

And many false prophets shall rise, and shall deceive many.

And because iniquity shall abound, the love of many shall wax cold.

But he that shall endure unto the end, the same shall be saved.

And this gospel of the kingdom shall be preached in all the world for a witness unto all nations; and then shall the end come.

Matthew 24:1-14

BE NOT DECEIVED

Notice what Jesus warns us in verse 4: **Take heed that no man deceive you.** In other words, He is saying, "Be careful that no man leads you into error."

When we think about being deceived, we think somebody is going to give us an obvious deception. But that is not how it works. The worst kind of deception in the world is the type that looks true. Realize this: Satan will not come at God's people with something so obvious. He will use something that only looks like the truth. So Jesus was saying, "Be careful not to be led into error."

Have you ever been led into error?

You have to be able to recognize the true Word of God. Maybe somebody did write a good book, but should you just automatically swallow the whole doctrine shared by that author in his book? You have to be careful and know how to spit out the bones. Let me give you an example.

Have you ever eaten mullet fish? When eating mullet fish, you can't just start chewing on it. You have to be careful to spit out the bones. I always heard that you should eat bread along with that kind of fish.

Well, here is the solution to getting rid of any spiritual bones that get caught in your throat: eat the Bread of Life. That will remove those bones. That's what I am doing by feeding you the Bread, God's Word. Then you will be able to fight against bones getting stuck in your throat.

So Jesus says we have to be careful that we don't let somebody lead us off into error.

SOME CLAIM, "FOLLOW ME — I'M ANOINTED!"

Jesus goes on in verse 5 of Matthew 24:

For many shall come in my name, saying, I am Christ; and shall deceive many.

We think Jesus is warning us to look out for those people who come and say, "I am Jesus Christ." But that isn't what He means here.

We miss a great revelation when we don't translate the word *Christ*. That isn't Jesus' last name. *Christ* means Messiah,[1] or the Anointed One.

In other words, Jesus is saying: "Many shall come and say, 'Follow me — I'm anointed!' They will claim to be anointed, but they shall deceive many."

I see this happening today. People will say, "I am the Anointed One." Then they will do something spectacular to try to win people's

---

[1]James H. Strong. *Strong's Exhaustive Concordance*. Compact Ed. (Grand Rapids: Baker, 1992), "Greek Dictionary of the New Testament," p. 78, #5547.

confidence. They will prophesy over you for an hour, really spinning your wheels with their little circus act; and before you know it, you will be floating off into the realm of deception. But you have to look at the fruit coming to you as a result of that ministry. Has there been a change in your life for the better?

BE NOT TROUBLED

Then Jesus says in verse 6, **Ye shall hear of wars and rumours of wars**, but the advice He gives in the midst of verse 6 is, **see that ye be not troubled**. He said in John 14:1, **Let not your heart be troubled**. So, we are responsible to see that we be not troubled.

Isn't that interesting? Right in the middle of trouble, God says, **see that ye be not troubled**. He is warning us today: "All these things will be happening around you, but in the midst of all the reports coming over the airwaves, see that you be not troubled."

The only way to avoid being troubled is by getting established in God's Word. So, how do you do that? By meditating in the Word until that truth becomes established in your heart.

If your heart isn't established in God's Word, you will find yourself yielding to trouble. So, pay the price by spending time in God's Word. Let it get down in your heart. Then your heart will be fixed, trusting in the Lord. (Psalm 112:7.)

Jesus goes on in verse 6: **for all these things must come to pass, but the end is not yet.** There are certain things that will come to pass. So, understand that, as the world gets darker, the Church will get lighter.

BUT DIVISIONS WILL COME

Now notice verse 7. Realize that Jesus is talking here about division. He says:

For nation shall rise against nation, and kingdom against kingdom....

He begins this verse with these words: **For nation shall rise against nation**. The word *nation* comes from the Greek word *ethnos*. This is where we get our word *ethnic*, which we use to describe the cultural differences of races and tribes of people. *Ethnos* means a race, a tribe, a non-Jewish one, a Gentile.[2]

Jesus was really saying: "For ethnic group shall rise against ethnic group, with one kingdom and its beliefs rising against another kingdom and its beliefs."

We can see this happening throughout history, can't we? And it is happening all over the world today. We find races rising up against other races, with one group of people fighting another group of people and killing one another because of their ethnic differences.

Look at what is going on in some of the European countries today, and has been going on for years. That is exactly what we are seeing in the old country of Yugoslavia, now known as Bosnia-Herzegovina: one ethnic group has risen against another ethnic group.

In the Far East, the Chinese are still against the Japanese for what happened in the past; and in Korea, it's one side against the other side.

Then here in America, there are extremes, particularly the blacks against the whites.

But we have the same kind of thing happening among Christian groups. Various denominations are rising against one another, and some ministries are trying to exalt themselves above other ministries.

There is a spirit of division at work in the world. We are about to see a spirit of separation and a spirit of racism like this planet has never known.

---

[2]Strong, "Greek Dictionary of the New Testament," p. 25, #1484.

But don't get sad. As the Church of Jesus Christ, we are in this world but not of it. (John 17:14,15.) We operate by a different system. We have come out of darkness into the marvelous Light. (1 Peter 2:9.) My objective is not to warn the world of this great problem of racism, but to make sure this spirit of division does not continue to invade the Church, the Body of Christ.

Now we could sit around and say, "Well, let's just not talk about it." But that is not the way to solve this serious problem.

A spirit of division is being used by Satan to invade the Church because he knows this is the time for a great outpouring of God's power. The devil is trying his best to stop this great outpouring by using division and separation to magnify differences within the Body of Christ. But I declare to you now: this time it won't work — God has the solution!

THE RESULTS OF DIVISION

Let's look again at Matthew 24:7:

For nation shall rise against nation, and kingdom against kingdom: and there shall be famines, and pestilences, and earthquakes, in divers places.

Now notice there is a colon after the phrase *kingdom against kingdom*. Jesus is pointing out what happens as a result of division and separation. He goes on:

...and there shall be famines, and pestilences, and earthquakes, in divers places.

First, there shall be famines. Now this does not necessarily mean a lack of food. Famine could mean the failure to receive a complete nourishment required in order to have certain things.

If the devil can cause ethnic groups to rise up against one another, that will hinder the feeding of the Gospel and the nourishment it provides. So, division and separation are deadly tools used by the devil.

Any time during history when there were wars, there were, first of all, divisions and separations that took place among the people. These were always divisive instruments used by the devil to cause the problem that led to the war. As a result, the people rose up and started fighting against one another.

The second thing Jesus mentions in this verse that happens when division takes place between ethnic groups is pestilence. I see this as something morally evil and destructive. What happens when pestilence comes in? It literally eats away and destroys.

Then the third result of division Jesus gives is earthquakes, which are symbolic of chaos and confusion. An earthquake is a violent shaking or convulsion in which there are vast openings in the earth that can sometimes swallow up whole cities.

Remember, in verse 4 of Matthew 24 Jesus said, "Be careful that you be not deceived," and in verse 11 He said, "Many false prophets shall rise, and many people shall be deceived." The earthquake, or the violent shaking of division, will open doors and allow things inside that could and should have been kept outside. Everything that can be shaken will be shaken, and that which remains shall remain.

SATAN'S ATTACK AGAINST RECONCILIATION

Jesus prophesies in verse 8:

All these are the beginning of sorrows.

Notice what He says in verse 9:

Then shall they deliver you up to be afflicted, and shall kill you: and ye shall be hated of all nations (ethnic groups) *for my name's sake.*

Now look at verse 10:

And then shall many be offended, and shall betray one another, and shall hate one another.

When division and separation come, when people begin to divide and rise up against one another, Jesus describes in this verse what happens among them. He says:

1. Many are offended.

2. They will betray one another.

3. They will start hating one another.

Would you agree with me that all of this appears to be an attack upon reconciliation in the Body of Christ? The devil is trying to take advantage of all the troubles going on to prevent us from operating in the ministry of reconciliation.

WHAT IS RECONCILIATION?

To reconcile means to restore to union and friendship after disruption or estrangement has taken place; in other words, after something has happened to mess up that relationship. It means to adjust or settle differences or quarrels which may still exist between two people, because their differences have never been satisfied or settled.

To restore to union means that separation has taken place. You cannot "re-store" something unless it has first been stored. To repeat means to say it again. You can't say it again unless you have said it in the first place. So something has to happen.

When we are trying to restore to union, that means union has been broken. Something has come in to mess up things — to challenge friendship and relationship.

Another definition of to reconcile is to remove apparent discrepancies. This means your adjustment, your restoration, will thoroughly change something.

Unfortunately, this is not the kind of adjustment Christians are famous for. Many say, "I can forgive that person, but I will never forget what he did." Then there is still a discrepancy.

Now if that's how you feel, I have to be honest with you and say I understand where you are coming from. Let me show you something that we honor, not higher than God's Word, but at least on the same level as the Word.

The word *reconciliation*, which is just an extension of the root word *reconcile*, means the renewal of friendship.

Let's say you have a relationship with another person, and the two of you are strong friends. But then something happens, and you just can't get a revelation of renewal to make it new again. Maybe you both reach the point where you just put up with each other, because as Christians you are required to operate in love.

RECONCILIATION TAKES MERCY

Reconciliation is the renewal of friendship after disagreement, after enmity. Literally, it is knowing how to take an enemy and make him your friend. It is coming into agreement after seemingly being opposite or inconsistent.

Reconciliation is to be merciful, which is a big word. When we talk about being merciful, what are we saying? The Bible says we are to show mercy to others as our heavenly Father has shown mercy towards us. (Luke 6:36.)

Think about how God has shown mercy towards us. He did it even when we had messed up, when enmity was being displayed by us.

The Bible says carnality is enmity with God. (Romans 8:7.) So when we have involved ourselves in carnality, which created enmity, we have to repent before God. When we do that, He forgives us and renews the friendship just like it was before we had committed that offense. Somehow we humans, preachers included, have had a difficult time doing this towards one another.

Suppose you and I were the closest and best of friends, but we had a disagreement. We got into a fight or argument and messed up our friendship. To reconcile means I must go to you and do whatever is necessary to bring us back together and to restore us to the way we were before we were separated.

That is reconciliation — to restore, to renew, to fix the problem, to dissolve the wall of partition between us, to be willing to come back together at all cost, to be merciful towards others as God has been merciful towards us.

THE GOSPEL IS THE WITNESS TO ALL

The good news of the Gospel is found in Matthew 24:14. Jesus says:

> *And this gospel of the kingdom shall be preached in all the world for a witness unto all nations* (ethnic groups)*; and then shall the end come.*

Jesus says we are to take the Gospel into all the world — where people have risen up against one another. In the midst of all this trouble — all this division, all this separation — we are to share the Gospel of the Kingdom.

We know there is a real problem of racism in the world. There are blacks who don't understand whites and whites who don't understand blacks. But how does God plan for us to handle it? What does He want us to focus on? What is the answer?

The only way to defeat racism is by discovering the foundation for unshakable faith — faith that won't be moved by the solicitation to divide and separate.

We won't be able to overcome racism or division in our homes, in our families or in our society until we understand what our covenant is all about. Let's take a closer look at some of the things going on in our society we thought were all right, to determine whether or not we should make changes.

THE FIRST STEP IS TO UNDERSTAND FAITH

Our first step in this study will be to look at what I believe is the foundation of our faith. I also believe it is something that some Christians have let slip: a real understanding of the law of faith.

We will be covering several passages of Scripture, going from one point to another, to lay this foundation. I promise you, this teaching will speak to you in truth. If you will tune in to the anointing, it will begin to work inside your heart. It is something that will absolutely change your life.

CHAPTER 2

The Law of Faith

Let's look first in the book of Romans, chapter 3. The apostle Paul writes:

To declare, I say, at this time his righteousness: that he might be just, and the justifier of him which believeth in Jesus.

Where is boasting then? It is excluded. By what law? of works? Nay: but by the law of faith.

Therefore we conclude that a man is justified by faith without the deeds of the law.

Romans 3:26-28

Then in verse 31 Paul says:

Do we then make void the law through faith? God forbid: yea, we establish the law.

Now anytime I teach on faith, there are some people who say, "Well, I've heard that before." But faith doesn't come by what you have heard. You could have heard the truth before and still not be walking in it. Faith comes by hearing, not by having heard. (Romans 10:17.)

FAITH — A WAY OF LIFE

Let's look now at Habakkuk, chapter 2, verse 4:

Behold, his soul which is lifted up is not upright in him: but the just shall live by his faith.

In Matthew 18:16 Jesus says it is out of the mouths of two or three witnesses that every word is established. So let's look at some other verses of Scripture that coincide with this statement in Habakkuk.

First of all, Romans 1:17 says:

For therein is the righteousness of God revealed from faith to faith: as it is written, The just shall live by faith.

Who shall live by faith? The just.

Who are the just? The born-again children of God who are baptized, Holy Ghost filled and fired up. The just are now the righteousness of God. They have been born out of darkness and into the marvelous Light, and they have been declared righteous. (1 Peter 2:9; 2 Corinthians 5:21.)

According to the Bible, the just have a new way of living. What is the way the just person shall live? By faith. Galatians 3:11 says:

But that no man is justified by the law in the sight of God, it is evident: for, The just shall live by faith.

Faith, then, is a way of life.

We don't just decide to live by faith when we are in trouble. Did you know you were going to have trouble? Some people have misunderstood this. They thought that when they lived by faith, they wouldn't have any trouble; but that's a lie straight from the pit of hell. When you live by faith, trouble will come and try to take your faith from you. That's why you need to really live by your faith, instead of just acting on it every now and then.

Hebrews 10:38 says:

Now the just shall live by faith: but if any man draw back, my soul shall have no pleasure in him.

Do you think God may be trying to tell us something here? In four Scripture verses, we have seen that **the just shall live by faith**. So, as we can clearly see, faith is a way of life.

LAWS TO LIVE BY

If you are born in the United States of America, you are required to live by the laws, rules and regulations that have been set up here. You are expected to attend school for 12 years, but you may go even further. You are taught subjects such as economics, geography and civics, where you learn about our government and how its judicial system operates. You are expected to live successfully in this society by following its rules.

The same principle applies when you are born again: you enter into the new society of the spirit world. Now, just attending church doesn't automatically make you born again. You have to decide in your heart to accept Jesus as Lord and Savior of your life. Once you do that and are born again, you go from spiritual darkness into the marvelous Light of the Gospel. Your next step is to learn how to exist in that new society by living a new life in Jesus.

We all know how to exist in the old society of darkness and sin. Many of us who are now believers in Jesus Christ can remember what it was like to live in sin. We smoked marijuana, snorted cocaine and drank a lot of alcohol. But when we got born again, we stepped out of that darkness into the marvelous Light. Then we had to learn the laws, rules and regulations that operate in this new society called Light.

You see, I couldn't go from darkness to Light and then walk in that Light the same way I had walked in darkness. I couldn't talk in the Light the way I had talked in darkness, or act in the Light the way I had acted in darkness. I am not the same as when I was living in that darkness; I am now a new creation, a new species of being, that never existed before. (2 Corinthians 5:17.)

The problem is, many times when we take that step out of darkness into the marvelous Light, we aren't motivated to go right into the Word of God. Instead of studying the Bible and learning how to pray and believe God for ourselves, we look at other Christians to see how they do it. Then we act like them. By doing so, we can easily make the mistake of following after someone who is still praying a bunch of doubt and unbelief.

FAITH REQUIRES ACTION

There is a story about a man who had been trekking across the desert. He saw an oasis far away, so he headed toward it. Finally, when he got there, he just collapsed.

A church group had stopped over for a rest, and they saw the weary traveller stagger in. A doctor on hand examined the man and discovered he was dying of thirst. What is the cure for a thirsty man? Water. So they revived him, set him in a chair and put water in front of him.

When the man saw that water, he said, "I believe if I drink this water, I will not die."

Then with a little more conviction, he said, "I believe it with my heart and say it with my mouth that if I drink this water, I will not die."

Then he got more excited and, with much more conviction, said, "I believe and say that if I drink this water, I will not die!"

He just kept saying, "I believe it." But then he fell over dead.

Now let me ask you a question: Were the words spoken by that man true or false?

Of course, they were true. The cure for a man dying of thirst is water. So, what he was saying was absolutely true. Yet he died.

Why?

Because he never acted on what he believed.

Faith is like the drinking of that water. You can't just believe it; you have to act on it — you have to do it. Faith is acting out what you believe. But if you haven't heard about it, if you haven't read about it, if you don't know what is in the Bible for you to believe, how are you ever going to act on it?

So, what is faith and how does it work?

WHAT IS FAITH?

Hebrews 11:1 says:

Now faith is the substance of things hoped for, the evidence of things not seen.

The first point I want you to understand is that faith has nothing to do with your senses.

This verse begins with these two words: **Now faith**. Faith is always now. God always abides in the eternal now. He is a "right now" God.

When God told Moses to go before Pharaoh and to lead the children of Israel out of bondage in Egypt, Moses asked, "But who will I say sent me?" God answered, **I AM THAT I AM...say unto the children of Israel, I AM hath sent me unto you** (Exodus 3:14).

God is saying, "I am whatever it is you need in your life." If you are sick, He says, "I am your Healer." If you are in bondage, He says, "I am your Deliverer." When you need a way out, He says, "I am the Way." When is God all these things to you? *Now!* So, faith is now.

Hebrews 11:1 says, **Now faith is the substance**. So, faith is a substance. But it isn't a tangible, physical substance that we can see. We know by the rest of this verse of Scripture that faith is unseen, but it's still a substance.

Now faith is the substance of things hoped for, the evidence of things not seen.

Hebrews 11:1

Faith is the substance of *what?* Of things. It is the substance of all physical things and all spiritual things. So, what am I saying?

Let's consider a podium as an example. Physical material is responsible for creating a podium. But whatever physical material was used to build the podium, faith is the spiritual substance which created that physical substance in the beginning. So, faith is the substance of *all* things.

Now let's go a little deeper in our study.

TWO REALMS OF EXISTENCE

Existing right now are two worlds, two realms: the physical world, where physical matter exists, and the spiritual world, where spiritual matter exists.

Once we step over into the spiritual world by accepting Jesus as our Lord and Savior, we are given authority over spiritual matter. (Ephesians 6:10-12.) There, we are able to see and touch what we can't see and touch in this physical world. So, that other world is real. In that world are things which faith is responsible for creating.

In Hebrews, chapter 11, we see that faith is the substance of things. Let's read on in verse 3:

Through faith we understand that the worlds were framed by the word of God, so that things which are seen were not made of things which do appear.

In other words, things we can see were made of things we cannot see.

John 1:1-3 says:

In the beginning was the Word, and the Word was with God, and the Word was God.

The same was in the beginning with God.

All things were made by him; and without him was not any thing made that was made.

Verse 3 says all things were made by God, and John 4:24 says, **God is a Spirit.** That means all spiritual things and all physical things come from God Who is a Spirit. So, the spirit world is the parent over this physical world.

In Genesis, chapter 1, we can read about the beginning as we know it. But God didn't come out of the beginning; He is too big for the beginning. The beginning came out of God. Anything that exists now started with God — the great I AM, El Shaddai.

WORDS — GOD'S FAITH CONTAINER

Now as we have seen in Scripture, faith is the substance of things, and everything was made by God. If we put those two Scriptures together, faith had to be in God for things to be made, because faith is the substance of those things. So, faith was in God.

Then one day God decided to put things into motion. But He needed a spiritual container, something that would dig down into His heart, be filled with the power within Him and then be released. He came up with words as that spiritual container. Jesus said, **The words that I speak unto you, they are spirit, and they are life** (John 6:63). Only words can dig deep into a man's heart, yet come out and affect this natural world. Let me give you an example.

Suppose I looked at you and said, "You good-for-nothing, dirty dog — I hate your guts!"

Which part of you would be hurt by those words — your physical body or your heart?

Your heart, of course.

But if I were to hit you over the head with a baseball bat, would that hurt your heart or your head?

Your head — and a big knot would come up to prove it.

Words create atmosphere. Have you ever been in a place after someone had spoken harsh words? You can just feel the atmosphere.

In the book of Genesis God decided to put His faith in the container of words. He saw darkness, so He said, "Light in Me, be!" The words He spoke contained the faith needed to produce that light. God put substance in the vehicle of words.

So, what is that telling us?

GOD'S WORD IS GOD'S POWER

We aren't to speak what we see all the time; we are to speak what God's Word says.

When we see trouble, we are to speak victory.

When we see sickness, we are to speak health.

When we see darkness, we are to speak light.

Realize that the devil can't prevent you from living a life of faith anymore. Since faith is in the container of words, God equates those words to Himself.

Think about it. If you know what kind of car I drive and you see me in my car, you wouldn't say, "There goes (the name of the car)." You would simply say, "There goes Pastor Dollar." You have equated me with that brand of car. Why? Because my car contains me, and you are seeing me when you see that container.

Now let's look again at John 1:1 and see what it says about words:

In the beginning was the Word, and the Word was with God, and the Word was God.

God put Himself in those words. He put His life and His power in those words. Hebrews 1:3 says He upholds all things by the Word of His power. Why does God's Word say that? Because the Word *is* His power.

FAITH EQUALS THE WORD

When you hold the Bible in your hand or rest it in your lap, you have the power of God right there with you. John 1:3 says:

All things were made by him; and without him was not any thing made that was made.

Because the Word is God and God is the Word, we can now read John 1:3 this way:

*All things were made by **the Word**; and without **the Word** was not any thing made that was made.*

Now let's look again at Scripture and read it with new knowledge. Everything we have ever learned about healing and deliverance, we learned from the Word. We know faith is in God's Word, but we can't see His faith because it's an unseen substance. However, if we put faith in words and write them down, we can look through the eyes of the Word and see that faith. So, let faith equal the Word of God.

Everywhere in Scripture that we find the word *faith*, let's change it to *the Word of God*.

Hebrews 11:1 would read:

Now the Word of God is the substance of things hoped for, the Word of God is the evidence of things not seen.

Habakkuk 2:4, Romans 1:17, Galatians 3:11 and Hebrews 10:38 would read:

The just shall live by the Word of God.

So, how shall the just live?

By the Word of God.

When you live by God's Word, you are living by faith. When you live by faith, you are living by God's Word. God's faith is in His Word.

I live by God's Word. I conduct my finances by His Word. I treat my wife by His Word. I raise my children by His Word. I treat my employees by His Word. Everything I do is by the Word of God. The Word is my constitution for living. So, I don't live the way I used to live. I now have a new set of laws: the law of faith.

SPIRITUAL WORLD — SPIRITUAL BLESSINGS

Look carefully at this:

Through faith we understand that the worlds (both physical and spiritual) *were framed by the word of God.*

Hebrews 11:3

This verse says we understand through *what*? Faith.

It says we understand *what* was framed? The worlds.

It says the worlds were framed by way of *what*? God's Word.

So, what was the substance used to frame the worlds? Faith.

What was the vehicle that delivered the faith? Words.

Here is what this verse is saying:

Worlds were framed, or assembled, with the substance of faith that was delivered by the Word of God.

Anything you need in the physical world was framed and assembled with the substance of faith delivered by the Word of God. When you get in God's Word, you have what you need to frame and assemble anything you might need in this physical world. If everything in this physical world has been born from the spirit world — and it has — then we must learn to operate in the spirit world.

Ephesians 1:3 says God has **blessed us with all spiritual blessings in heavenly places in Christ.** Ephesians 2:6 says God has **raised us up together, and made us sit together in heavenly places in Christ Jesus.**

Where is Christ Jesus, the Anointed One?

In heavenly places.

Where are we, the believers?

In Christ Jesus.

There are spiritual blessings in heavenly places in the Anointed One; and because the Anointed One is in us and we are in Him, spiritual blessings are in us, too.

Jesus said, "If I be lifted up from the earth, I will draw all men unto Me." (John 12:32.) He didn't tell us to lift ourselves up; we are to lift Him up. He is the Word, so when we lift up that Word, we are lifting up Jesus.

I have made up my mind to never stop preaching this Word. Sometimes people come to our church wanting to see something spectacular. But to them I say, "Go to the circus."

You have to understand something: I am a believer and I live by God's Word. I don't need to see a miracle. I am a miracle going somewhere to happen. You don't need to show me something spectacular; I already believe God. Jesus is the King of kings and the

Lord of lords. He went to hell for my sins and rose on the third day for me. So, I am a believer in Him!

Let's look at Romans 1:16:

For I am not ashamed of the gospel of Christ: for it is the power of God unto salvation to every one that believeth; to the Jew first, and also to the Greek.

Now the word *gospel* means good news. It says in this verse that the good news is the power of God. As I had mentioned earlier, Hebrews 1:3 says God is **upholding all things by the word of his power**. So, get hold of that. People try to find God's power in some physical manifestation, something like goose bumps or jerking. But that isn't where God's power lies. God's power is in His Word.

Some people may ask, "Pastor Dollar, why haven't I been operating in the power?" Because you haven't been living in His Word. Maybe you don't feel you need all of that. But you have in your possession the power of the awesome God in the form of the Bible, so you have to allow that Word to go into your heart and then come out your mouth.

LAW OF FAITH ESTABLISHED

Let's look again in Romans, chapter 3, at our Scripture text. God has done all He will ever do about healing, about our finances, about the devil. His Word is His will, and God has already said yes to a life of faith. Verse 27 says:

Where is boasting then? It is excluded. By what law? of works? Nay: but by the law of faith.

Faith is a law, and a law is something that works the same way every single time. Take the law of gravity, for instance. It works the same, regardless of who operates it. If you don't believe it works for you, just climb to the top of a building and step over the side. You will find out right away exactly how gravity works!

The Law, which we find in the Old Testament, was a law of works; and by working it, the people were made righteous. But, the New Testament law was established when Jesus gave Himself on the cross as the sacrificial Lamb. Under this new Law, righteousness comes not by works, but by faith. Romans 3:31 says:

> *Do we then make void the law through faith? God forbid: yea, we establish the law.*

Now we know this verse isn't talking about the Law of the Old Testament; it is in the same context and is still talking about the law of faith. What is the apostle Paul saying here? That they are establishing the law of faith.

Let's go further into this topic now by looking in Romans, chapter 8. Paul is making a progression when talking about this law of faith.

CHAPTER 3

FAITH IN YOUR HEART

I believe the apostle Paul is referring to the same law of faith in Romans 8 that he talked about in Romans, chapter 3. Romans 8:6 says:

For to be carnally minded is death; but to be spiritually minded is life and peace.

What does it mean to be carnally minded? It means to be fleshly minded. (This topic will be dealt with more fully in a later chapter.)

What does it mean to be spiritually minded? Unfortunately, people seem to get really spooky when they talk about being spiritual.

Walking in the Spirit does not mean you will be walking somewhere in the air. Jesus said, **The words that I speak unto you, they are spirit, and they are life** (John 6:63). To be walking in the Spirit is to be walking in God's Word, to be doing the Word, to be living the Word.

To be spiritually minded, then, is being Word-minded. God's Word says, **Thou wilt keep him in perfect peace, whose mind is stayed on thee** (Isaiah 26:3).

How can you keep your mind stayed on Him? Through the Word.

THE CARNAL MIND VS. THE LAW OF GOD

Look at Romans 8:7:

Because the carnal mind is enmity against God: for it is not subject to the law of God, neither indeed can be.

What is the Law of God? The law of faith. The carnal mind cannot be subject to the Law of God, which is the law of faith.

The Law of God declares God **calleth those things which be not as though they were** (Romans 4:17). But the carnal mind says, "You can't do that, because I can't feel it."

The Law of God declares, **What things soever ye desire, when ye pray, believe that ye receive them, and ye shall have them** (Mark 11:24). But the carnal mind says, "If I can't see it, I won't believe it."

Now listen: be very careful when preachers try to cause God's Word to make sense. It isn't sense; it is faith.

A minister told me one time, "You ought not give expecting to receive; you ought to just give because you love God."

Another preacher said, "When you get sick, you aren't supposed to get healed all the time; somebody has to die."

These statements bothered me, so I asked the Lord about them.

Those preachers are saying we aren't supposed to expect a reward from God, we are just supposed to love Him. That would be like saying to a farmer, "You go and plant some corn seed, because you love the ground; just don't expect a harvest." That would be foolish!

Maybe you walk around saying, "I'm serving the Lord, and it doesn't matter if He never rewards me; I'll serve Him anyway."

Now I am serving Him too, but it does matter. Why? Because He said He would reward us. Anytime God's Word doesn't come to pass, we have a problem on our hands.

God's Word is true. If what He has said is not manifested in our lives, we need to go back and consider where we went wrong. The fault always lies somewhere with us — never with God. The problem is, we haven't done what is necessary to bring that Word into manifestation in our lives.

The Word says that by His stripes we are healed and that a man will reap whatsoever he sows. (Isaiah 53:5; Galatians 6:7.) God said it; I didn't. Since God's Word is the only thing that can get me in contact with the God I cannot see, it is vitally important that He does what He says. Besides, Jesus said, **It is your Father's good pleasure to give you the kingdom** (Luke 12:32).

Hebrews 11:6 says, **He that cometh to God must believe that he is, and that he is a rewarder of them that diligently seek him.** To believe God is not the Rewarder is to believe He does not exist.

We must believe God is the Rewarder. He wants to reward us because He knows we are a people of motivation. He says, "If you will keep My commandments, I will bless you coming in and bless you going out." (Deuteronomy 28:1,6.) God wants to motivate us to do what He tells us to do.

He wants to reward us by giving us the hundredfold return when we plant seed in His Kingdom. (Mark 10:29,30.)

He wants to heal our bodies when we stand on the Word for healing. (Isaiah 53:4,5; Psalm 103:1-4; 1 Peter 2:24.)

He wants to rescue us when we come to Him for deliverance. (Deuteronomy 28:1-14; Psalm 112; 1 Peter 5:6-9.)

God gives us these promises in His Word, and it is important that His Word comes to pass as He said it would. (I didn't say it — He did.)

You should say, "I give because I love the Lord." To love the Lord is to keep His commandments: seedtime and harvest, sowing and reaping, giving and receiving.

Now let's zero in on another important point.

FAITH WORKS IN THE HEART, NOT IN THE HEAD

The law of faith is like the law of gravity. The problem is, some people don't work the law of faith. The law of gravity is mandatory; it will make you obey. But the law of faith is optional.

According to Romans 8:7, the carnal mind cannot operate in God's law of faith. Faith works in the heart. Now when I use the word *heart*, I don't mean the heart that pumps blood; I mean the spirit of man. Man is a spirit, he possesses a soul (his mind, will and emotions) and he lives in a physical body.

Faith is a spirit force. It doesn't work in man's head; it works in his spirit, or heart. To have the faith of God in you, with the reality of it being produced, it must be digested in your spirit, or in your heart.

Mental assent, on the other hand, works in the head, so mental assent is not faith. A person with mental assent will say, "That's in the Bible." But ask him if he really believes it, if it is truth at work in his life, and he will say, "Well, no; it really isn't." Then God's Word is not yet in his spirit; it is only in his mind.

Faith won't work in the head, and this is where so many people get in trouble. They think all they have to do is say it 300 times. But if it never gets down in their heart, they are only operating by a formula, and they have missed the entire point. For faith to work, it must be developed.

I will use weight lifting as an example. Let's say I have been benching weights for five or six years and have worked up to 350 pounds. Now suppose you have never lifted weights in your life; but after watching me for a while, you think, *I believe I can do that.* So, you get under the bench, assuming you can lift it because it's there.

But the moment you take that bar down off the rack, you cry out, "Help!"

The problem is, a lot of people make the mistake of taking Scripture and trying to run with it. They don't realize their faith muscle has not been developed to handle that much weight. So, they have to start working their faith muscle. Jesus said, "Be faithful over a few things, and you will be ruler over many things." (Matthew 25:21.)

Don't wait until you get cancer before you try working your faith muscle. Start by standing against a sneeze or minor pain in your head. This time, skip the Tylenol. Not that faith is or is not in the Tylenol. You can take the Tylenol and pray over it if you want to. Just remember, taking the medicine is not what brings healing to you; God is still the Source of your healing.

FAITH COMES BY HEARING

Now there are some shortcuts you can take to really get faith in your heart. For instance, if you speak God's Word out your mouth, faith will come more quickly. Romans 10:17 says, **So then faith cometh by hearing, and hearing by the word of God.** Faith comes by hearing God's Word.

Think about this for a moment. It doesn't say you have faith by hearing; it says faith comes by hearing. You don't have pizza by calling; you have pizza by paying the delivery boy when he comes. You have faith when you act on what you hear. But you gain potential by hearing.

I know faith comes when I hear God's Word. When God speaks, every Word is filled with a sufficient amount of faith to bring itself to pass. That's why God says, **So shall my word be that goeth forth out of my mouth: it shall not return unto me void, but it shall accomplish that which I please, and it shall prosper in the thing**

whereto I sent it (Isaiah 55:11). God's Word must be spoken in order to be heard.

FAITH ALWAYS TALKS THE END RESULTS

How can I hear unless it is spoken? But I have more faith in what I say myself than in what I hear you say. When I speak the Word of God and you hear it, faith will come to you. But when you start speaking the Word for yourself, faith will surely come. There is a difference in the degree of power when it comes out of your own mouth.

The Bible indicates that believing is seeing. Faith will always talk the end results instead of what exists at present. Some people assume something will happen, not because they have faith in God's Word, but because of what happened to some other person. But we can't put our faith in what happened to another person; we must have faith in God's Word. Faith is seeing in the spirit realm what the Word has promised when it is not yet manifested in the natural realm.

What we speak out our mouths sets the cornerstones of our lives. Words can deceive us. The words we speak transmit either faith or fear.

THE POWER OF THE TONGUE

As the old saying goes, "Sticks and stones may break my bones, but words will never hurt me." But that isn't true. Proverbs 11:3 says, **the perverseness** [AMP: crookedness] **of transgressors shall destroy them.**

God's Word is His will for man, and man's word should be his will towards God. Proverbs 18:21 says:

Death and life are in the power of the tongue: and they that love it shall eat the fruit thereof.

Which do you love — death or life? If you love death, you will eat the fruit of death. If you love life, you will eat the fruit of life.

We must get our spoken words in line with the Word of God. When God's Word is conceived in the heart, then formed with the tongue and spoken out the mouth, it becomes a spiritual force releasing the ability of God.

We can also conceive and speak other words. For instance, the words of the devil conceived in the heart and spoken with the mouth will release the ability of the devil.

God's laws are involved with confessions and the principles of faith. Hearing the Word causes faith in that Word to come. This spiritual force is also released out of your mouth when you speak God's Word. It actually releases God's ability.

Why does this method work? Why does Joshua 1:8 tell us to meditate in the Word day and night and not to let the Word depart from our mouth? Why does God want us to keep the Word on our lips?

Notice that when we speak words, we also hear what we say. Now I am going to talk to you on medical terms and on spiritual terms.

In the physical body, there are two sets of ears: the outer ear and the inner ear. I have read that the inner ear (inside the head) is made up of bone structures which feed our voice directly into our human heart. This is why the words we speak ourselves are even more important than the words spoken to us by others. Our own words affect our whole being.

JESUS SPOKE THE FATHER'S WORDS

Have you ever wondered why it is impossible for God to lie? Because every time God opens His mouth and speaks, He releases faith in those words, and everything He speaks will automatically come to pass. His words are filled with enough faith to bring them to pass.

Have you ever wondered why Jesus had such great faith? Because He spoke only what He heard His Father say. In John 12:49,50 Jesus said:

For I have not spoken of myself; but the Father which sent me, he gave me a commandment, what I should say, and what I should speak.

And I know that his commandment is life everlasting: whatsoever I speak therefore, even as the Father said unto me, so I speak.

Jesus was telling us: "I say only what the Father says. The Father's words are already filled with faith, so if I speak what He has already said, I will see what the Father sees."

YOU TOO CAN SPEAK
FAITH-FILLED WORDS

Let's look now at Jesus' words in John, chapter 8:

I have many things to say and to judge of you: but he that sent me is true; and I speak to the world those things which I have heard of him.

When ye have lifted up the Son of man, then shall ye know that I am he, and that I do nothing of myself; but as my Father hath taught me, I speak these things.

And he that sent me is with me: the Father hath not left me alone; for I do always those things that please him.

...If ye continue in my word, then are ye my disciples indeed;

And ye shall know the truth, and the truth shall make you free.
John 8:26,28,29,31,32

Again, Jesus was telling us, "I only say what My Father says." So, what happens when you say what Jesus has said? You too are saying what the Father has said.

Jesus said: "If you continue in My Word, like I continue in My Father's Word, you will know the truth like I know the truth. As it made Me free and kept Me free, it will make you free and keep you free."

Notice what makes you free: the Word that came out of the mouth of God being filled with His faith.

When I really saw this truth for the first time, I learned where I had been missing it: I was more concerned about speaking my own words than about speaking God's Word that was already filled with faith.

Faith that is in the Word gets into your spirit when you speak it. The Bible doesn't say, "Faith cometh by *reading*." It says, **Faith cometh by *hearing*** (Romans 10:17). However, for those who are hearing impaired, faith comes to them through sign language, and through Braille to those who are blind. But to hear it, it must be spoken in whatever form of language necessary to get into your spirit. So, keep what the Word of God says before you.

In Luke, chapter 4, Jesus only responded to the devil by speaking the words of the Father. He said, **It is written, That man shall not live by bread alone, but by every word of God** (v. 4).

WRITE GOD'S WORD ON THE TABLE OF YOUR HEART

Now, if you can get God's faith words down in your heart, or in the soil, it will grow. Proverbs 3:3 says:

Let not mercy and truth forsake thee: bind them about thy neck;
write them upon the table of thine heart.

This says you are to write them on your heart. But why must you do that?

Let's look at Habakkuk 2:2. I know when we read or hear this verse from Habakkuk, we immediately think about vision, but it says something much more powerful than that:

And the Lord answered me, and said, Write the vision, and
make it plain upon tables, that he may run that readeth it.

The Hebrew word translated "vision" here in the *King James Version* is translated "revelation" in the *New International Version* (NIV). That means words that have come out the mouth of God.

Write the vision, and make it plain upon tables, that he may
run that readeth it.

For the vision [or that word which is written on tables] *is yet*
for an appointed time, but at the end it shall speak, and not
lie: though it tarry, wait for it; because it will surely come, it
will not tarry.

Behold, his soul which is lifted up is not upright in him: but the
just shall live by his faith.

Habakkuk 2:2-4

Now what is this saying?

That for you to see power in your life, it has to be written on the table of your heart. God will read the writing on the heart because He doesn't weigh a man by his outer appearance, or by the flesh; He weighs the heart of a man. God is looking at your heart and is weighing you by your heart. In the Old Testament, the people looked at David and saw a shepherd boy; but God, reading David's heart, saw a king. Hallelujah!

We only have one dilemma: How do we write things on the table of our hearts so that God can read it and run with it?

THE PEN OF A READY WRITER

Psalm 45:1 says:

My heart is inditing a good matter: I speak of the things which I have made touching the king: my tongue is the pen of a ready writer.

Notice this verse says, **my tongue is the pen of a ready writer.**

Have you been writing sickness and disease on your heart? Have you been writing doubt and unbelief on your heart? Have you been writing defeat on your heart? If so, I say to you, hear ye the word of the Lord!

Begin to write God's Word on your heart. Write salvation on your heart. Write deliverance on your heart. Write victorious living on your heart. Then speak that Word of God out your mouth.

When you do this, God will weigh your heart; He will read your heart. When He sees His Word there on your heart and then hears it come out of your mouth, He will bring it to pass in your life. When it is on your heart, then spoken by faith out of your mouth, it shall surely come to pass, because your tongue is the pen of a ready writer.

It's time we start speaking the right things. When we read and study the Word of God, we are writing it on our heart. Then when it gets in our heart and comes out of our mouth, the ability of God comes forth.

Everything God ever does, He does by speaking His Word. We should learn to be like Him. Now I didn't say we are God. God is sovereign; we are not. We should always be subject to Him. But I want to be like my spiritual Daddy. I want to talk like Him and walk like Him.

YOUR TONGUE CAN DECEIVE YOUR HEART

Now notice James 1:26:

If any man among you seem to be religious, and bridleth not his tongue, but deceiveth his own heart, this man's religion is vain.

If this man does not bridle his tongue, what he believes is in vain, for his tongue will deceive his heart.

Now why would the tongue deceive the heart? Because the tongue speaks words which are picked up by the inner ear and are fed directly into the heart, or spirit.

Your heart, or spirit, assumes you want what you are speaking. So your tongue can deceive your heart into believing the words you speak are exactly what you want. Your spirit will say, *Let's find a way to bring it to pass.*

If you say with your mouth, "I'm sick," your spirit says, *I believe that's what he wants.* So, your tongue is deceiving your heart. You said it, but is it really what you want?

In Matthew 12:34 Jesus says:

...for out of the abundance of the heart the mouth speaketh.

You are a product of your words. Where you are right now is a result of the seeds you have planted in the past.

But I'm going to say what I want to say!

Then say it. But by doing so, you will remain in the bondage you have created with your own words.

When God weighs your heart, what does He see, a shepherd or a king? Again, Psalm 45:1 says, **my tongue is the pen of a ready writer.** So, what has your pen been writing?

THE NEXT STEP OF STUDY: ABRAHAM

This concludes the first step of our foundation of faith. Our next step will take us into a study about Abraham, the father of our faith. We will learn more about faith by looking into the subject of covenants. We will begin by looking at Abraham in the New Testament, then trace him back to his beginnings in the Old Testament.

God wants His people to stop looking at each other through the flesh. In the eyes of God, there are only two races: believers and unbelievers. You are either one or the other.

CHAPTER 4

ABRAHAM AND HIS COVENANT WITH GOD

Let's begin in the book of Romans, chapter 4. Speaking of Abraham, verse 18 says:

Who against hope believed in hope, that he might become the father of many nations, according to that which was spoken, So shall thy seed be.

This is interesting. It says, **that he might become the father of many nations**. This is a hidden revelation of what was to happen when God made Abraham the father of many nations. Not just the father of his own tribe, but the father of many ethnic groups.

HE WAS STRONG IN FAITH

Now let's find out how God would take this one man, Abraham, and make him the father of many ethnic groups. Describing Abraham, it says:

And being not weak in faith, he considered not his own body now dead, when he was about an hundred years old, neither yet the deadness of Sarah's womb:

He staggered not at the promise of God through unbelief; but was strong in faith, giving glory to God;

And being fully persuaded that, what he had promised, he was able also to perform.

Romans 4:19-21

The first point we notice in this passage about Abraham is in verse 19, where it describes him as **being not weak in faith**. What is "weak faith"? Faith that always considers the circumstances in a situation.

Then verse 20 says he **staggered not at the promise of God through unbelief; but was strong in faith**; and verse 21 says he was **fully persuaded**.

How would you like for someone to say you are not weak in faith, but have strong faith; that you stagger not at the promises of God and are fully persuaded?

I want you to realize, though, that Abraham wasn't always like this. He didn't always have strong faith. He wasn't always fully persuaded when the Word of God came forth.

So, what occurred to make a difference in his life? What made him become the strong man of faith we preach about and talk about today?

We need to trace Abraham back to his beginnings and find out what happened in his life. Let's see him before he walked in this strong faith, before he stood strong and staggered not at the promise of God. By discovering what happened to him, we can learn how to apply it in our own lives and produce the same results.

Let's go now to the book of Genesis, the book of beginnings. I want to be sensitive to the reader who may have never heard or read teachings like this before. I don't just take it for granted that you already know this story. I want to make sure I cover it so that everyone will understand it.

First of all, you need to realize that before this man became known as Abraham, his name was Abram. At this point in his life, Abram was involved in idolatry; he was a worshipper of the moon. So, he had been a stranger to God. Now God knew Abram, but Abram didn't really know God.

GOD APPEARS TO ABRAM

Let's look in Genesis, chapter 15:

After these things the word of the Lord came unto Abram in a vision, saying, Fear not, Abram: I am thy shield, and thy exceeding great reward.

And Abram said, Lord God, what wilt thou give me, seeing I go childless, and the steward of my house is this Eliezer of Damascus?

And Abram said, Behold, to me thou hast given no seed: and, lo, one born in my house is mine heir.

And, behold, the word of the Lord came unto him, saying, This shall not be thine heir; but he that shall come forth out of thine own bowels shall be thine heir.

Genesis 15:1-4

I want you to get a picture of what God does here: He tells Abram to come outside and look towards heaven. Continuing in verse 5, it says:

And he brought him forth abroad, and said, Look now toward heaven, and tell the stars, if thou be able to number them: and he said unto him, So shall thy seed be.

And he believed in the Lord; and he counted it to him for righteousness.

And he said unto him, I am the Lord that brought thee out of Ur of the Chaldees, to give thee this land to inherit it.

And he said, Lord God, whereby shall I know that I shall inherit it?

Genesis 15:5-8

This doesn't sound at all like the Abraham we have read about in Romans, chapter 4. Here, he is not walking in strong faith; he is staggering. In verse 8 he says, "I hear what You are saying, God. But I don't know how I will inherit this."

Now put yourself in Abram's shoes for a moment.

God comes to him with this dramatic introduction, saying: "Fear not, Abram. I am your Shield and your Great Reward. I will bless you and your name. I will give you seed that outnumbers the stars. I will give you land to inherit."

That must have blown Abram away. First of all, he really didn't know God. It was as if God came to him out of the blue, making promises of great things He would do for him.

AN EXAMPLE OF A CONTRACT TODAY

So that you can really relate to this, let me give you an up-to-date example. Let's say you are walking along in a shopping mall when, all of a sudden, a total stranger approaches you. He says: "Hello. I will give you a billion dollars, a Rolls Royce and the dog you've always wanted. All you have to do is meet me here at two o'clock tomorrow afternoon."

As you are listening, you think: *I sure hope this guy can do what he says. But I don't know about him. He doesn't look as if he has a lot of money, yet he comes up to me and makes all these promises.*

Now you will be working at two o'clock the next day. In fact, your boss has warned you that you can't leave work early anymore, because if you do, you will get fired. But, you were told that if you were to come back to the mall the next day, you would be given all those things. The entire time you are saying to yourself, *How will I know he's going to give me all that he says?*

Given these conditions, are you willing to leave your job and go to the mall the next day to meet a total stranger?

Some people might say, "Hey, I might as well; I don't have anything else to lose." But ninety-five percent of us wouldn't be willing to put our jobs on the line with that kind of a risk. We would be thinking, *I've never met that man. How do I know he isn't just playing with my mind? How do I know he'll actually do what he has promised?*

Now let's take the same situation and change the circumstances just a bit.

Let's say you are at the mall, and the stranger comes up to you carrying a legal contract in his hand. In that document are terms guaranteeing that he will give you the billion dollars, the Rolls Royce and the dog you have always wanted.

He has signed his name at the bottom of the contract, and it is properly sealed. All you have to do is sign your name on the dotted line. Would you be willing to do that?

Now, I am assuming this is an honorable contract. That means there is a guarantee that you will receive all that money, and you wouldn't need to work for minimum wage anymore. The chance is far greater that you would be willing to sign your name on that dotted line.

GOD'S COVENANT WITH ABRAM

But Abram doesn't have a written contract with God. He doesn't have anything that would bind those words from God, guaranteeing that he would get what had been promised. So he asks God this question: "How will I know that I will inherit it? Give me something solid, something binding, if You will."

Then God begins to answer him:

And he said unto him, Take me an heifer of three years old, and a she goat of three years old, and a ram of three years old, and a turtledove, and a young pigeon.

Genesis 15:9

You may be wondering, "What does a heifer, a goat, a ram, a turtledove and a pigeon have to do with getting what God promised?" Let's read on:

And he took unto him all these, and divided them in the midst, and laid each piece one against another: but the birds divided he not.

And when the fowls came down upon the carcases, Abram drove them away.

And when the sun was going down, a deep sleep fell upon Abram; and, lo, an horror of great darkness fell upon him.

And he said unto Abram, Know of a surety that thy seed shall be a stranger in a land that is not theirs, and shall serve them; and they shall afflict them four hundred years;

And also that nation, whom they shall serve, will I judge: and afterward shall they come out with great substance.

And thou shalt go to thy fathers in peace; thou shalt be buried in a good old age.

And it came to pass, that, when the sun went down, and it was dark, behold a smoking furnace, and a burning lamp that passed between those pieces.

Genesis 15:10-15,17

So, what was going on here? Verse 18 tells us:

In the same day the Lord made a covenant with Abram....

Abram had asked God a question: "Whereby shall I know that I shall inherit this land and have a seed that outnumbers the stars?"

God answered him by saying: "You understand a blood covenant; you live this way. So I will cut the covenant with you."

What, then, is a covenant? Let's define it.

A BLOOD COVENANT

A covenant is a pledge, a vow, a promise, a commitment between two or more parties to carry out the terms they have agreed upon. This covenant is established in blood and can only be broken by death.[1] So, this is a serious contract, a serious agreement. We are talking here about a blood covenant between God and Abram, as we read from Genesis, chapter 15.

When God said to Abram, "I will cut the covenant with you," that's when Abram became a believer. Abram was familiar with blood covenants; they were practiced all the time in the society in which he lived.

The first thing you do in a blood covenant ceremony is to recognize the need for a covenant. The covenant was designed for differences and for weaknesses. Let me give you an example to illustrate what Abram saw when God said, "I will cut the covenant with you," and why Abram was so convinced.

---

[1]Information taken from *Library of Universal Knowledge*, published by Consolidated Book Publishers, p. 171, "covenant."

AN EXAMPLE OF COVENANT

Let's say we have two families joining together by covenant: a family of farmers and a family of warriors.

The farmers know how to grow the best produce, but they don't know how to fight; so, because of that weakness, their food could be taken from them by an enemy.

The warriors are the best fighters in the land, but they don't know how to farm. Without food to eat, they won't be fighting for long.

Do you see why these two families should get together and talk covenant?

Because of their weaknesses.

When my wife and I were married, we each had strengths and weaknesses. Where I was strong and she was weak, I exchanged my strengths for her weaknesses. Where she was strong and I was weak, she gave me her strengths for my weaknesses. By joining together in our marriage covenant, we have eliminated all the weaknesses in our lives.

So it's important to note that a covenant is designed for strengths and weaknesses.

Now these two families, the farmers and the warriors, have a need to cut the covenant. One family can't fight; the other family can't grow their own food.

To form a covenant relationship, they must first come together and have lengthy discussions about the terms of the covenant and how they can benefit from one another.

This is an important aspect of marriage, because marriage is a covenant. Before getting married, a man and woman should have some lengthy conversations. They need to discuss how they each feel about life in order to really know about one another. She should discover before marriage that he doesn't want children. He should find out before the honeymoon night what she really looks like without all that makeup.

Now, once the terms of the covenant have been established between the farmers and the warriors, those two families announce that there will be a ceremony to bring them together in covenant with one another. They choose a ceremonial site, a place where the covenant will be cut; then they pick the best representative of each family — the best warrior in one group, the best farmer in the other group.

Before the ceremony, the two representatives in that covenant relationship go out and find an animal to be used as a covenant sacrifice. Then they bring it with them to the covenant site where the ceremony will take place.

They give their sacrifices a special cut, called a covenant cut. This incision is made straight down the spine, dividing the animal into two perfect halves. The two halves are then set opposite one another, where the blood can flow between them and mix together to form a walkway of blood.

Now they are ready to begin the ceremony.

EXCHANGES ARE MADE

The two family representatives walk in the blood, quoting to one another their vows that are based on the terms they have agreed upon. The fighter swears to the farmer: "I promise, you will never have to fight your own battle again." The farmer swears to the fighter: "I promise, you will never have to do your own farming again."

Then they come to the middle of that walkway of blood. They cut their hand or wrist where their blood will begin to flow, and they bind their hands together so that their blood will mingle. Then they raise their hands, clasped together, to show the two families that their blood has merged.

After the blood has mingled, there are some exchanges that take place in the ceremony. When you are in covenant, you are no longer an individual.

First, there is an exchange of coats, representing authority. The authority of the farmer is now put on the warrior, and the authority of the warrior is now put on the farmer.

We could see this really well in our society today if, for instance, a captain in the Air Force and a lieutenant in the Army were to exchange coats with one another. They each would be given authority in that other branch of service.

After the farmer and warrior have exchanged their coats, or their authority, then when people look at them, they see something new. Looking at the farmer, they no longer see just a farmer; they now see a farmer-warrior. Looking at the warrior, they no longer see just a warrior; they now see a warrior-farmer.

The next exchange they make is with their weapons. The farmer gives his tool to the warrior; the warrior gives his weapon to the farmer. This exchange demonstrates how they have swapped their power and ability with one another.

Then the last exchange that takes place is an exchange of names. They are no longer just the warrior family and the farmer family. They are now the warrior-farmer family, with each family representing the other.

The final part of the covenant ceremony that takes place is included in many marriages today; we call it a reception. The two families come together to eat bread and drink from the cup.

By holding up the bread, they are reminding one another, "I swear to you over this bread that, before I let you starve, I would let you eat my flesh."

By holding up the cup, they are saying, "I swear to you that before I let you be defeated in battle, I would fight for you and die for you."

Then they give the consequences for breaking their covenant by saying to one another, "I remind you that you are bound to keep this covenant; if you ever break it, we will hunt you down from generation to generation until you are found and killed." This shows just how serious they are about keeping their covenant.

Now if people today would keep this part of their covenant of marriage, they would be more careful about getting married right away. If the father of the bride would be pledging to the groom, "You misuse my daughter and you will be hunted down from generation to generation until you are found and killed," then the groom might think long and hard about whether he really wanted to get married.

PEOPLE HAVE A FEAR OF DIFFERENCES

Again, let me state that a covenant is designed for differences and for weaknesses. The problem is, people in our society are taught to be afraid of the differences and weaknesses in other people.

When we see somebody who was raised in a different culture or background from us, our instinct is to be afraid of that person. We aren't familiar with his culture, so we fear him because of those differences.

We know there are differences between blacks and whites. Here is an example:

A white man, meeting a black man, says to him, "Hello, how are you doing today?"

A black man, meeting a white man, says to him, "Yo, man, what's up?"

If they would come together, they could talk about their different ways of greetings and salutations. Then it wouldn't be long before the white man is saying, "Yo, man, what's up?" and the black man is saying, "Hello, how are you doing today?" That's learning how to be all things to all people.

Another example of differences between the white man and the black man is when they are singing. The white man claps on the first beat; the black man claps on the second beat. Imagine what would happen if they came together and cut a covenant: then when they started clapping, they wouldn't miss a beat! Why? Because once they have entered into covenant, they would be taking up for one another's weaknesses.

ABRAM MAKES A COVENANT SACRIFICE

Let's go back to Scripture and read one more time about Abram's sacrifice in Genesis, chapter 15. It makes more sense now when Abram asked the question, **Whereby shall I know that I shall inherit it?** (v. 8). Again, God said to him:

Take me an heifer of three years old, and a she goat of three years old, and a ram of three years old, and a turtledove, and a young pigeon.

Genesis 15:9

Can you see what Abram was doing? He was making a covenant sacrifice.

Verse 10 says he took the heifer, the goat and the ram, **and divided them in the midst, and laid each piece one against another**.

Verse 12 says Abram fell out under the power of God.

THEN GOD ENTERS THE COVENANT

All of a sudden, God started having a lengthy conversation with Abram.

In Genesis 15:13 God described how Abram's seed would be a stranger in a land and be afflicted there for four hundred years. This is what happened when God's people were in bondage to Egypt.

Then God said in verse 14, "But I will judge those whom My people serve, and I will cause My people to come out of bondage with great substance."

God was talking about the mass exodus of the children of Israel, walking out of bondage from Egypt. That's when the wealth of the wicked was handed over to the Israelites. Then God opened the Red Sea for His people to cross, and He closed those waters, killing all the Egyptians to whom His people had owed money. These were the terms of the covenant. (See Exodus 12:31-41; 14:5-31.)

Now look at Genesis 15:17:

And it came to pass, that, when the sun went down, and it was dark, behold a smoking furnace, and a burning lamp that passed between those pieces.

This verse says it was **a smoking furnace, and a burning lamp that passed between those pieces.** *The Amplified Bible* calls it **a flaming torch.**

I submit to you that it was not an angel or some other individual who walked between those two pieces. I believe it was God Almighty. The smoking furnace and the burning lamp, which Abram saw, was God coming from His throne in heaven and walking in that blood with man. God Almighty had come to cut the covenant with man, so this covenant is now between God and man. Glory to God!

THE COLOR OF LOVE

AN EVERLASTING COVENANT ESTABLISHED
BETWEEN GOD AND MAN

Now I want us to look in Genesis, chapter 17. This gives more scriptural support to what I have just demonstrated to you. Genesis 17:1 says:

> *And when Abram was ninety years old and nine, the Lord appeared to Abram, and said unto him, I am the Almighty God; walk before me, and be thou perfect.*

When Abram heard the words, "I am the Almighty God," his Hebrew ear heard it like this: "I am El Shaddai, the many-breasted one. I am your nurse, your provider. I am more than enough, all you will *ever* need." Then God said:

> *And I will make my covenant between me and thee, and will multiply* [or increase] *thee exceedingly (v. 2).*

In response to this, Abram fell on his face, and God talked with him, saying:

> *As for me, behold, my covenant is with thee, and thou shalt be a father of many nations (v. 4).*

Then comes the name exchange, with Abram's name being changed to Abraham. God said:

> *Neither shall thy name any more be called Abram, but thy name shall be Abraham; for a father of many nations* [ethnic groups] *have I made thee.*
>
> *And I will make thee exceeding fruitful, and I will make nations of thee, and kings shall come out of thee.*
>
> *And I will establish my covenant between me and thee and thy seed after thee in their generations for an everlasting covenant....*

> Genesis 17:5-7

Something has changed. This is no longer just a covenant between God and Abraham. Now it is a covenant between God, Abraham and Abraham's seed. And it is a covenant that has a will, because it can be inherited by the seed of Abraham. God goes on to say:

> *And I will establish my covenant between me and thee and thy seed after thee in their generations for an everlasting covenant, to be a God unto thee, and to thy seed after thee.*
>
> *And I will give unto thee, and to thy seed after thee, the land wherein thou art a stranger, all the land of Canaan, for an everlasting possession; and I will be their God.*
>
> *And God said unto Abraham, Thou shalt keep my covenant therefore, thou, and thy seed after thee in their generations.*
>
> *This is my covenant, which ye shall keep, between me and you and thy seed after thee; Every man child among you shall be circumcised.*
>
> *And ye shall circumcise the flesh of your foreskin; and it shall be a token of the covenant betwixt me and you.*
>
> Genesis 17:7-11

In that day, circumcision was the token, or sign, of the covenant, just as the wedding ring is a token, or sign, of the marriage covenant today. But we no longer have to circumcise the flesh of the foreskin; now it is the circumcision of the heart that counts in our covenant with God through Jesus Christ.

God is serious about this covenant. In Psalm 89:34 He says, **My covenant will I not break, nor alter the thing that is gone out of my lips.** Psalm 111:5 says God **will be ever mindful of his covenant.** God does not intend to break this covenant; He just won't do it. Hebrews 6:13 says, **When God made promise to Abraham, because he could swear by no greater, he sware by himself.**

Now let's look at Abraham in Genesis, chapter 22, and see how the covenant affected his life. He is no longer Abram, the idolater, the stranger of God; he is now Abraham, the covenant-friend of God, the father of many nations. Because he has entered into covenant with God, he does not talk or respond to God the way he once did.

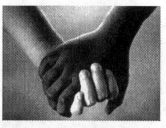

CHAPTER 5

GOD'S COVENANT IS COLOR-BLIND

ABRAHAM TOLD TO SACRIFICE HIS SON

And it came to pass after these things, that God did tempt Abraham, and said unto him, Abraham: and he said, Behold, here I am.

And he said, Take now thy son, thine only son Isaac, whom thou lovest, and get thee into the land of Moriah; and offer him there for a burnt offering upon one of the mountains which I will tell thee of.

And Abraham rose up early in the morning, and saddled his ass, and took two of his young men with him, and Isaac his son, and clave the wood for the burnt offering, and rose up, and went unto the place of which God had told him.

Genesis 22:1-3

Now what was God telling Abraham to do?

To take his son and to offer him as a sacrifice.

This certainly could not have been an easy task for Abraham. God knew Isaac was Abraham's only son whom he loved, but God told him to go and kill his son, using him as a sacrifice. Now watch how this covenant man operated:

Then on the third day Abraham lifted up his eyes, and saw the place afar off.

And Abraham said unto his young men, Abide ye here with the ass; and I and the lad will go yonder and worship, and come again to you.

Genesis 22:4,5

Did you catch what this covenant man said? Abraham knew exactly what God had told him to do. He was to take his son and offer him as a sacrifice. But Abraham had said to those men, "We are going there to worship God for a while; then the boy and I will come back to you."

Abraham had already made up his mind that God would have to do something. Why? Because he remembered the night God had taken him outside and had told him to look up towards the heavens. God had asked him if he could number the stars, then had said, **So shall thy seed be** (Genesis 15:5).

Abraham also knew that for his seed to outnumber the stars, it would have to come out of Isaac. God had to either raise Isaac up from the dead, or choose another sacrifice to take Isaac's place.

ABRAHAM'S STEP OF FAITH

Abraham had already made up his mind. He was saying to God: "You can either give me a sacrifice or raise my son from the dead. It makes no difference to me. I will be satisfied any way You want to bless me."

Knowing God couldn't lie, Abraham was saying to Him: "I know something has to happen. I can remember the day You walked in between those two halves. I can remember the day You swore by Yourself, because there was no one greater to swear by. I know You will fulfill Your promise. Therefore, I will just obey Your Word and let You do the rest."

So often, we may not understand what is happening in our lives, but we have the Word of God and the blood of Jesus. We may not know how God will get us out of our situation, but we know He will do something. We can say like Abraham, "Any way You bless me, Lord, I will be satisfied."

Now let's continue with Abraham's step of faith:

And Abraham took the wood of the burnt offering, and laid it upon Isaac his son; and he took the fire in his hand, and a knife; and they went both of them together.

And Isaac spake unto Abraham his father, and said, My father: and he said, Here am I, my son. And he said, Behold the fire and the wood: but where is the lamb for a burnt offering?

Genesis 22:6,7

Many of us believe Abraham had much faith, but Isaac must have had it, too. He needed faith that his father wasn't getting senile and that God really had told him to do this.

Look how this covenant man responded to his son, even in the midst of what seemed to be trouble:

And Abraham said, My son, God will provide himself a lamb for a burnt offering: so they went both of them together.

And they came to the place which God had told him of; and Abraham built an altar there, and laid the wood in order, and bound Isaac his son, and laid him on the altar upon the wood.

And Abraham stretched forth his hand, and took the knife to slay his son.

And the angel of the Lord called unto him out of heaven, and said, Abraham, Abraham: and he said, Here am I.

And he said, Lay not thine hand upon the lad, neither do thou any thing unto him: for now I know that thou fearest God, seeing thou hast not withheld thy son, thine only son from me.

And Abraham lifted up his eyes, and looked, and behold behind him a ram caught in a thicket by his horns: and Abraham went and took the ram, and offered him up for a burnt offering in the stead of his son.

And Abraham called the name of that place Jehovah-jireh: as it is said to this day, In the mount of the Lord it shall be seen.

Genesis 22:8-14

Let me show you what was going on here.

THE COVENANT RELATIONSHIP
BETWEEN GOD AND ABRAHAM

There is a covenant law, a covenant rule, that says whatever one covenant partner requests of another, then he must be willing to do the same and to take it a step further. We are talking now about the covenant relationship between Almighty God and Abraham.

Abraham had an inner image of the covenant, but we don't really see it in this chapter of Genesis. Let's look in the book of Hebrews. There, we will get a better picture of what was going on inside Abraham when all of this was happening.

It had to be a real test for Abraham to offer up his son. But notice he didn't stagger one bit.

Why?

Because he knew he had a covenant with God. He knew God could not lie. God had told him he would be the father of many nations, so he was just acting on God's Word.

Now watch this carefully. I want you to get a picture of what Abraham did here as we bring to a close this teaching on the foundation of faith. But I want to make sure you understand it before we go further in dealing with this subject of division.

A PARALLEL BETWEEN FATHER ABRAHAM AND FATHER GOD

By faith Abraham, when he was tried, offered up Isaac: and he that had received the promises offered up his only begotten son,

Of whom it was said, That in Isaac shall thy seed be called:

Accounting that God was able to raise him up, even from the dead; from whence also he received him in a figure.

Hebrews 11:17-19

Verse 19 AMP reads like this:

For he reasoned that God was able to raise [him] up even from among the dead. Indeed in the sense that Isaac was figuratively dead [potentially sacrificed], he did [actually] receive him back from the dead.

Abraham was using his imagination here. He had a blueprint drawn in his mind's eye. He saw a picture of Isaac being figuratively put to death and potentially already sacrificed. So, he could see Isaac being raised from the dead.

Abraham was saying: "In order for me not to walk in fear, I have to see Isaac figuratively dead as a sacrifice." He had already declared with his mouth that God was going to provide a sacrifice, and he wanted to cover the other area too. He began to potentially see his son already sacrificed so that in his own imagination, figuratively seeing his son dead, he could get a picture of God raising his son from the dead.

Abraham knew God had to either raise his son from the dead or provide another sacrifice, so he got an image of God raising up his son.

But we know God provided a sacrifice. We also know, if God was going to ask Abraham to do this with his own son whom he loved, God Almighty would have to be willing to do the same with His Son.

So, there is a parallel in this situation I want you to see:

On one side, there is Abraham, the father of many nations; on the other side, there is God, the Father of all creation.

On one side, there is Isaac, the son of Abraham; on the other side, there is Jesus, the Son of God.

On one side, we see Isaac being put on the altar to be made a sacrifice; on the other side, we see Jesus made a sacrifice by being put on the cross.

God saw what Abraham was doing by faith, so He responded, saying:

"Hold on, little covenant partner. I see your vision. I see the picture. So, keep your son; he can live. Now you step aside. As your Covenant Partner, I am willing to take it the rest of the way. I will take the image you had of Me raising your son from the dead and let them crucify My Son.

"I will allow My Son to die on the cross and be buried, but then on the third day, I will use the vision you had of Me raising your son from the dead to raise My Son from the dead. I will raise up My Son as King of kings and Lord of lords. Then I will be able to raise all of mankind. When I raise Jesus, when I lift Him up, then He can lift you up where you belong."

Now I want you to see God coming to your rescue, saying: "Step aside, little covenant partner. Be still; I am in covenant with you. Let Me fight the rest of your battle."

All of this happened because of the covenant relationship between God and man.

GOD'S PROMISE IS TO *ALL* WHO BELIEVE

We can see something very interesting in Hebrews 9:16,17. I want you to realize you can be brought into this covenant, regardless of what color your skin may be. This Scripture says:

For where a testament is, there must also of necessity be the death of the testator.

For a testament is of force after men are dead: otherwise it is of no strength at all while the testator liveth.

Let's say your Uncle Jim is a billionaire and has included you in his will. He is the testator, so you cannot receive what was left to you in his will until he dies. The only way force can be added to that will is by death.

That is what happened when Jesus died on the cross. He wrote a will, then died so that you could receive what had been left you in His will. But He did something no other testator has ever been able to do: not only did He die to add force to the will so that you could obtain what was left you, He also rose from the grave to make sure you had received what had already been left to you by Him.

Then I asked this question: "Well, Lord, as a black man, where do I fit in here; and where does a white man or member of any other ethnic group fit into this whole situation?"

Let's look in Galatians, chapter 3. I advise you strongly to read this entire chapter, but we will begin in verse 24:

Wherefore the law was our schoolmaster to bring us unto Christ [the Anointed One], that we might be justified by faith.

But after that faith is come, we are no longer under a schoolmaster.

For ye are all the children of God by faith in Christ Jesus.

For as many of you as have been baptized into Christ [the Anointed One] have put on Christ [the Anointed One].

Galatians 3:24-27

As a result of our putting on the Anointed One and His anointing, notice what the apostle Paul says in verse 28 of this chapter:

There is neither Jew nor Greek, there is neither bond nor free, there is neither male nor female: for ye are all one in Christ Jesus.

Remember in Genesis 17:7 God said to Abraham:

I will establish my covenant between me and thee and thy seed after thee in their generations for an everlasting covenant, to be a God unto thee, and to thy seed after thee.

God was saying, "Abraham, I am making you the father of many ethnic groups." Here is how He did it: He cut a covenant with Abraham and swore on that covenant to his seed.

ONE COVENANT — ONE PEOPLE — ONE IN CHRIST

Now whether we are black-skinned, white-skinned, red-skinned, yellow-skinned or brown-skinned, when we become believers in Jesus, we can put on Christ. So, regardless of what we may look like on the outside, when we put on Christ, we become Abraham's seed. Then Galatians 3:29 says:

And if ye be Christ's, then are ye Abraham's seed, and heirs according to the promise.

As believers in Jesus Christ, the Anointed One, we become Abraham's seed. And as Abraham's seed, we are heirs according to the promise!

That means there is neither black nor white when we are in the Anointed One.

There is neither Chinese nor Japanese when we are in the Anointed One.

There is neither Mexican nor Korean when we are in the Anointed One.

There is neither Baptist nor Methodist, neither Word of Faith nor Charismatic, when we are in the Anointed One.

Jesus made a way so that people of all colors and all ethnic groups could become the seed of Abraham.

So, how do we become Abraham's seed?

By being born again, going from darkness into His marvelous Light, being declared the righteousness of God.

No matter what color our skin may be, we are Abraham's seed. That means everything God promised to Abraham also belongs to you and to me. God's blessing is no longer to the Jew; it is now to us, the believers in Christ Jesus.

In God's eyes, there is no longer a black man, or a white man, or a Jewish man, or a Mexican man, or an Oriental man. We all are covenant people. The blood of Jesus is red, and we are one in Christ because of His covenant.

THE RIGHTS OF A COVENANT MAN

There were certain things I was not allowed to do as a black man, because of the ills and prejudices in society. But when I was born again through Jesus Christ, I became a covenant man.

There were certain things a white man couldn't do. But he became a covenant man through Jesus Christ.

We now are able to do all things through Christ Jesus, the Anointed One, Who strengthens us with the might we need to get the job done.

To the covenant man, Isaiah 54:17 says:

No weapon that is formed against thee shall prosper; and every tongue that shall rise against thee in judgment thou shalt condemn. This is the heritage of the servants of the Lord, and their righteousness is of me, saith the Lord.

What does that mean? Just this:

Whatever God had promised to Abraham, we born-again believers can say, "Me, too!"

When God said to Abraham, "I will be a blessing to you and make your name great," then we covenant people, as the seed of Abraham, can say, "Me, too!" (Genesis 12:2.)

When God said, "I will take sickness out of the midst of thee," we covenant people can say, "Me, too!" (Exodus 23:25.)

When God said, "You will be blessed coming in and blessed going out," we covenant people can say, "Me, too!" (Deuteronomy 28:6.)

When God said, "I will cause you to walk upon high places," we can say, "Me, too!" (Deuteronomy 33:29.)

When God said, "Your enemies will come against you one way, but I will cause them to flee before you seven ways," we can say, "Me, too!" (Deuteronomy 28:7.)

Everything God promised to Abraham in the covenant was promised to him in blood. That means, because of Jesus' blood, we can stand boldly and say, "Me, too!" Again, as it says in the Scripture, **If ye be Christ's, then are ye Abraham's seed, and heirs according to the promise** (Galatians 3:29).

The exciting thing about this is — whether you are a white man, a black man, a red man, a yellow man or a brown man — as long as you are a covenant man, Abraham's blessings are yours!

Because I am in Christ, I am not just a black man; more than that, I am a covenant man, an heir to God's promises. That means things are changed now. As a black man, I can have a white brother, because we have one blood in the family — the blood of Jesus.

This is truth, and it will change your life. Are you willing to receive it from God?

Let's look now in Ephesians, chapter 2:

For we are his workmanship, created in Christ Jesus [the Anointed One] *unto good works, which God hath before ordained that we should walk in them.*

Wherefore remember, that ye being in time past Gentiles in the flesh, who are called Uncircumcision by that which is called the Circumcision in the flesh made by hands;

That at that time ye were without Christ [the Anointed One], *being aliens from the commonwealth of Israel, and strangers from the covenants of promise, having no hope, and without God in the world:*

But now in Christ Jesus [the Anointed One] *ye who sometimes were far off are made nigh by the blood of Christ.*

For he is our peace, who hath made both one, and hath broken down the middle wall of partition between us;

Having abolished in his flesh the enmity, even the law of commandments contained in ordinances; for to make in himself of twain one new man, so making peace;

And that he might reconcile both unto God in one body by the cross, having slain the enmity thereby:

And came and preached peace to you which were afar off, and to them that were nigh.

For through him we both have access by one Spirit unto the Father.

Now therefore ye are no more strangers and foreigners, but fellowcitizens with the saints, and of the household of God.

Ephesians 2:10-19

We are no longer strangers. We are fellow citizens.

Let's turn up the notch a little bit now and dive right into this issue of division, separation and racism within the Body of Christ. I will show you some things from God's Word concerning division. The world's view calls it discrimination; the Bible calls it division. The world's solution for discrimination is integration; the Bible's solution for division is reconciliation.

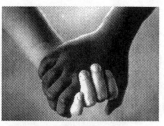

CHAPTER 6

IS CHRIST DIVIDED?

Let's read First Corinthians 1:11,12 where the apostle Paul says:

For it hath been declared unto me of you, my brethren, by them which are of the house of Chloe, that there are contentions among you.

Now this I say, that every one of you saith, I am of Paul; and I of Apollos; and I of Cephas; and I of Christ.

Then in verse 13 Paul asks these questions:

Is Christ divided? was Paul crucified for you? or were ye baptized in the name of Paul?

In other words, Paul is asking believers: Why are you identifying with somebody who didn't do anything for you? Why are you identifying with your natural heritage when it is because of Jesus that you now have a spiritual heritage, which is eternal life with God?

He is saying, "If you be Christ's, then are you Abraham's seed — but was Christ divided?"

A SPIRIT OF DIVISION AMONG US

There is an issue occurring today that is being covered up, especially by pastors. They just don't seem to want to deal with it, so they act like it doesn't exist. I will give you an example:

A black man says, "I'm a Christian, I worship God and I really want to do what's right, but I hate the white man." Then a white man says, "I love the Lord and thank God for His many blessings, but I just can't deal with those black folks."

As a black man, I make it a point, every chance I get, to sit down and talk about this subject with other pastors.

On the surface, Christians say, "Let's just love one another." But how can we love one another when we have this subtle spirit of division among us?

The black man looks at the white man and thinks, *You act just like the typical white man.*

The white man looks at the black man and thinks, *Look at him — he's just like all the others.*

Neither of them will say this outwardly, but they will tell little jokes about it and just smile. They don't mind attending the same church sometimes — just as long as they don't have to do it all the time. But they certainly don't want their daughters to marry a man of another color. "After all," they say, "we can't be messing up the family line. We have to be careful to marry in our own kind."

But what do they mean by "our own kind"? Our kind is human. You know, a black horse never has a problem mating with a white horse. They each can be of a different color, but that doesn't stop them from producing another horse.

So, is Christ divided? I want us to look at this in First Corinthians, chapter 3. Now don't try to ignore this issue; and as you read this book, don't be thinking that you know somebody else who needs it. Think about how you yourself fit into this situation, about what needs to get right in your own life.

CARNALITY CAUSES DIVISION

And I, brethren, could not speak unto you as unto spiritual, but as unto carnal, even as unto babes in Christ.

I have fed you with milk, and not with meat: for hitherto ye were not able to bear it, neither yet now are ye able.

1 Corinthians 3:1,2

Paul is saying to these believers, "You weren't able to bear it then, and you still aren't able to bear it." Verse 3 tells us why:

For ye are yet carnal....

The word *carnal* here means fleshly.

Then he gives the reason members of the Body of Christ are still carnal and are not yet spiritual, and why they haven't yet received any promotion. Verse 3 continues:

...for whereas there is among you envying, and strife, and divisions....

Notice all of these are like cousins: envy, strife and divisions. You won't have one without the other. Where you see division, there will be strife and envying. Now look at the rest of verse 3:

...are ye not carnal, and walk as men?

Notice that the basis for the spirit of division is carnality. Verse 4 says:

For while one saith, I am of Paul; and another, I am of Apollos; are ye not carnal?

Paul is saying that when you look at folks through the flesh and determine their actions based on their color and their ethnic group, then you are being carnal.

The spirit of division and the spirit of separation are produced by that carnality.

GOD GIVES THE INCREASE

Who then is Paul, and who is Apollos, but ministers by whom ye believed, even as the Lord gave to every man?

I have planted, Apollos watered; but God gave the increase.

So then neither is he that planteth any thing, neither he that watereth; but God that giveth the increase.

1 Corinthians 3:5-7

Who are we without Christ? Nothing. As soon as we realize that we are nothing without Christ, the better we will be. But we have to be careful.

Even in intercession, man has a tendency to take credit for what God has done by saying, "Well, God did it because I'm an intercessor." We can thank God for our intercession, but we must give Him the credit and the glory for it. We could have prayed all night long, but if God didn't want to move, He wouldn't.

God says through Paul, "I gave the increase." He is saying, "One planted, one watered, but I made it happen. You saw an increase because of Me."

Now he that planteth and he that watereth are one: and every man shall receive his own reward according to his own labour.

For we are labourers together with God: ye are God's husbandry, ye are God's building.

According to the grace of God which is given unto me, as a wise masterbuilder, I have laid the foundation, and another buildeth thereon. But let every man take heed how he buildeth thereupon.

For other foundation can no man lay than that is laid, which is Jesus Christ [the Anointed One].

1 Corinthians 3:8-11

Who is Paul? Who is Apollos? Is Christ divided?

Now, let's turn the knob up just a little bit, and I will show you how these divisions happened. I want this to be settled in your mind.

WHAT ABOUT SKIN COLOR?

A number of books have been written on the subject of blacks in the Bible. It seems certain men of God feel that this is important. They say:

"We are writing this because it's important for black people to know they had their part in the Bible. They need to know that Adam and Eve were black. They need to know Jesus was a black man. This will help them to feel good about themselves and have some self-esteem."

Having seen pictures of both a white Jesus and a black Jesus, I have wondered about this, so I asked the Lord about it: "Lord, could some of us be guilty of entertaining itching ears by telling our people what they want to hear, rather than telling them what the Word says? Does that do me any good as a black man?"

Is it worth it to lie to folks about all of this just so they can have self-esteem? Wouldn't it be the same as preaching to itching ears for me to tell them what they want to hear, instead of telling them the truth?

I remember one time a man came up to me and said, "Brother Dollar, I saw you on Kenneth Copeland's television broadcast. I just felt so proud of you."

So, I asked him, "Did you hear what I said?"

"No. I just know that you're black, and I'm proud to be a black man like you."

After telling Brother Copeland about it, I asked him, "How do I handle something like that?"

He said: "Think about it. If some people are watching you just because you're black, then you could deceive them anytime. When they say they're proud of you, you should say to them: 'Then you require of me as a black man to preach nothing but the Word. I'm responsible to preach nothing but the Word. My being black and being on TV doesn't mean a thing.'"

You see, that man was only proud of me because of my color. That means I might be able to deceive him at any time, because he wasn't really listening to what I was saying.

So, what am I saying to you? If you trust somebody just because of his skin color and you don't really hear what he is saying, then you are setting yourself up to be deceived.

You ought to demand that your man of God preach you nothing but the Word of God. Don't be proud of me because I am a black man. Be proud of me because I am preaching God's Word.

Millions of Muslims have been deceived because they are only looking at skin color; they aren't hearing what is being said. God is a God of love, not a God of hatred. I don't care what color you are; God has never recommended that you hate anybody.

We have to be careful not to be led astray with this idea about who in the Bible is black.

Maybe you think everybody in the Bible is black because they were in Africa. If so, that means you have never been to Africa. I have, and I recognize that there are some Africans who look even darker than those who have the curly, woolly type of hair. Anyone in Africa is going to tan over time.

If you find out who in the Bible is black, that may only lead other people to seek their roots in the Bible. Thus, we will create a foundation for competitive jealousy. All this does is engender a bunch of questions like, "Why does he have to be black?" or "Why can't he be white?"

I wondered, "Lord, why are these men writing these books when You have specifically told us in Your Word not to do this?"

I will show you a couple of Scriptures that I hope will settle this question forever. It specifically tells us not to check into the past in order to find out what color somebody was in the Bible.

OUR SPIRITUAL HERITAGE

I heard one time that there was a preacher talking behind my back, saying, "Well, you know, it looks like Pastor Dollar has lost his identity."

No, Pastor Dollar hasn't lost his identity — he has finally found his identity. He now knows who he is in Christ!

There is a difference between natural heritage and spiritual heritage. As a black man, I didn't have much to inherit. Maybe I can't learn about who I am in the natural, but I have discovered who I am in God's covenant. When I became a covenant man, I inherited everything God had promised to Abraham. Now I know who I am: a covenant man who happens to be black. I am glad that I am black. And you should be glad no matter what color you are, whether black or white, red or brown.

I am glad everybody isn't the same color as I am and doesn't look like me. Our strengths come when we can join together as different races of people and begin to supply one another's needs.

It is exciting to me that we all can be in Christ, regardless of skin color. As soon as we recognize this truth, we will quit fighting one another.

AVOID ENDLESS GENEALOGIES

Let's look at First Timothy 1:3,4:

As I besought thee to abide still at Ephesus, when I went into Macedonia, that thou mightest charge some that they teach no other doctrine,

Neither give heed to fables and endless genealogies, which minister questions, rather than godly edifying which is in faith: so do.

Again, it says, **Neither give heed to fables and endless genealogies**.

What is a genealogy? It is an account or a synopsis tracing the descent of a person or family from an ancestor. It is the study of family history.

The apostle Paul is saying here: "Don't get involved in tracing back into history to find out who they were and what color they were. When you do that, as far as this Bible is concerned, it will only bring up questions rather than ministering godliness."

So, God didn't call His people to find out who among them was black and who was white.

Now maybe you want to go back and trace your family tree. That's fine. But don't do it as far as the Word is concerned. Don't try to trace your genealogy to find out who was black and who was white. If you waste all your time in the study of genealogy, there won't be time for you to get born again and be set free from the devil's devices. Instead, spend time studying God's Word. Learn to walk in the Spirit and not in the flesh.

Some black people have wasted a lot of their time asking all kinds of questions, such as whether Adam and Eve were black. As we have read in Second Timothy 1:4, Paul said that, rather than having all these questions occur, we should be preaching something that is edifying, which is in faith.

I don't care what color Adam and Eve were. All I know is, when Jesus died, He shed the blood of God. That blood was good enough to set all of us — blacks *and* whites — free from poverty, sickness and disease.

So, as Paul wrote in his second letter to Timothy: **Foolish and unlearned questions avoid, knowing that they do gender strifes** (2 Timothy 2:23).

Now the end of the commandment is charity out of a pure heart, and of a good conscience, and of faith unfeigned:

From which some having swerved have turned aside unto vain jangling;

Desiring to be teachers of the law; understanding neither what they say, nor whereof they affirm.

1 Timothy 1:5-7

PREACH LOVE, NOT GENEALOGIES

I want to read this passage from *The Amplified Bible*. It really nails down this point.

As I urged you when I was on my way to Macedonia, stay on where you are at Ephesus in order that you may warn and admonish and charge certain individuals not to teach any different doctrine.

Nor to give importance to or occupy themselves with legends (fables, myths) and endless genealogies, which foster and promote useless speculations and questionings rather than acceptance in faith of God's administration and the divine training that is in faith (in that leaning of the entire human personality on God in absolute trust and confidence) —

Whereas the object and purpose of our instruction and charge is love, which springs from a pure heart and a good (clear) conscience and sincere (unfeigned) faith.

1 Timothy 1:3-5 AMP

Do you know what Paul is saying here? That we have been called to preach love, not genealogies.

But certain individuals have missed the mark on this very matter [and] have wandered away into vain arguments and discussions and purposeless talk.

They are ambitious to be doctors of the Law (teachers of the Mosaic ritual), but they have no understanding either of the words and terms they use or of the subjects about which they make [such] dogmatic assertions.

1 Timothy 1:6,7 AMP

This really concerns me. Some men of God are creating division in the Body of Christ with their books about racism. I am not trying to solve racism in the world; I am only concerned about the Church.

My concern is that people are buying those books to find out who in the Bible was black, then going around telling folks they were that color. But the Bible tells us not to do that.

Paul says, "Don't get involved in something that will cause people to ask this question. Instead, preach love."

Do you know why?

Because when we all, as believers — people of every color — get to heaven, we will put on our new glorified bodies. We will no longer be as we are here on earth. We will be like Jesus. Why? Because the Bible says, **When he shall appear, we shall be like him; for we shall**

see him as he is (1 John 3:2). Jesus won't be regarded in the same way He was when He was here on earth.

DON'T BE LED ASTRAY

When God looks at believers, He no longer sees all the different races in the earth. The middle wall of partition has been taken down; it has been abolished. It's time that we in the Body of Christ recognize there is no separation any longer!

"Well, I want a picture of a black Jesus hanging on my wall."

"Well, I want a picture of a white Jesus hanging on my wall."

"Well, I want a picture showing Jesus with slanted eyes."

If you really saw what Jesus looked like on the cross, you wouldn't want such a picture hanging in your house. Isaiah 53:3,4 describes Him as being **despised and rejected of men; a man of sorrows, and acquainted with grief...stricken, smitten of God, and afflicted.**

The most revealing painting I ever saw of Jesus showed Him severely beaten and bruised; His body was so messed up that you couldn't tell what color He had been — it was just black and blue.

But then somebody might say, "See there — I told you He was black!"

Please don't be so easily led into error. Don't even get involved in it. Why? Because it takes the attention away from learning how to walk in love and puts it on what color people were back in Jesus' day. Does it really matter?

"Yeah, it does matter," you might say, "because black or white people need to know they were involved to build up their self-esteem."

Then they need to get saved!

SELF-ESTEEM IN JESUS

My self-esteem got built up immediately once I found out that I had delegated jurisdiction:

...that I am the head and not the tail, that I am above and not beneath. (Deuteronomy 28:13.)

...that I am more than a conqueror and an overcomer through Jesus. (Romans 8:37; 1 John 5:4,5.)

...that greater is He that is in me than he that is in the world. (1 John 4:4.)

I found out I have been given authority in His Word and power in His name, and I can be led by the Holy Ghost.

I found out who I am: a new creature in Christ. Old things have passed away and, behold, all things have become new. Glory to God! I am now a born-again child of God. (2 Corinthians 5:17.)

If you have accepted Jesus as Lord and Savior of your life, you have been given these blessings, too!

A NEW RACE OF BELIEVERS

I was talking to a white brother one day. He said: "You know, what I couldn't get as a white man, I now can get as a covenant man. I tried to be a successful white man, but I couldn't do it until I met Jesus."

That's the way I see it in my own life: What I could not get as a black man, I can now get as a covenant man.

Coming into covenant with God gives us the ability we didn't have before. When we operate in the ministry of reconciliation, we operate in a ministry that is anointed. When God gives us a ministry,

He gives us the anointing to carry out that ministry. We have to start telling folks about this truth.

I happen to be a black American, but more than that, I am a born-again, covenant-based believer in Jesus Christ. I belong to the family of believers, and I am running in a new race now.

I heard that one person, trying desperately to come up with a theology, told how the Bible says light came out of darkness, proving all whites came out of all blacks. That's the most ridiculous thing I have ever heard in my life! But people are teaching such things.

These are vainless, endless genealogies, which do nothing but engender strife and envy and questions. The Bible says we are to avoid them.

DON'T BE AFRAID OF DIFFERENCES

There is one thing I must say at this point: Don't be afraid of differences. I am not telling people to act as if I am not black.

As I heard one white person say, "Creflo, you are a good old boy; you don't even act like a black boy."

The fact of the matter is, whether I act like one or not, I am still black.

That person would say, "Well, we don't see him as black. We see him as one of ours."

I don't ask white people to see me, a black person, the same way they would see other white people. The fact is, I am different. I probably came up in a different situation. There even are black people who came up in different situations than mine.

So, don't be afraid of differences. Let them cause increase in your life. Just because something is different doesn't mean you ought to be afraid of it. You can reap great benefits by learning from people of other ethnic backgrounds.

I always wanted to have a friend from every ethnic group. I like hanging out with different people. I remember having a Christian brother who is Chinese. The things I learned from that culture gave me some balance.

Also, having spent time in Nigeria, I have been able to learn about that culture. I learned it is the custom for two friends there to hold hands as a sign of strong friendship. Now imagine two men in the United States walking down the street, holding hands. That might raise some questions as to their sexuality.

While in Nigeria, as I came out of the hotel, a brother in the Lord walked up and grabbed my hand. That was just too strange for me! So, for the rest of the trip, I walked around with my hands in my pockets.

But I have realized we can learn from differences.

Now imagine what would happen if a white church, a black church, a Korean church and a Mexican church all hooked up together once a year on New Year's Eve. That would be the truest representation of the Body of Christ. I believe God's anointing would really flow.

Remember, a covenant is designed for differences. So, don't be afraid of differences; learn to appreciate them.

AN EXAMPLE OF DIVISION

Let me give you an example of how easy it would be to create division among people.

Let's say when speaking to a church congregation I ask those who drive a Mercedes to stand. The moment they stand, we have created separation. Those who don't drive a Mercedes will sit there, looking around at those standing. That's when feelings of competitive jealousy, ill will and envy could start knocking on the door.

What happens next? Strife comes in.

People say, "I have the right to be fussy if I want to be. I can be downright mean if I want to be."

Anything to divide and conquer.

Then we have magnified our differences.

IT'S TIME FOR RECONCILIATION

Listen, I love my brothers and sisters in the Lord. I don't care what color they are. I still appreciate being a black man, with my kind of hair and my color of skin, but I also appreciate my white brothers. I am in covenant with men of other ethnic and racial backgrounds. I can stand arm in arm with a white man, because he is my covenant brother. We are in covenant together, and the world can't figure it out.

Let me tell you, God had a great cure for my prejudice: my wife and I adopted a white child. When people come up to me now and say, "You're a racist," I can say, "Well, I guess I am. There are a bunch of races in my family!"

As we were raising that white boy, there were a couple of times when he got into trouble because he almost thought he was black. Once while in a predominantly black gym, he asked one of the other players to pass the ball, using a racial slur for black. Those guys just looked at him. I said, "Greg, you have to remind yourself that, as a white person, you can't say that. Not everybody will understand."

When I was at a convention of national pastors, a preacher came up to me and said, "Pastor, all of my life I was the kind of person you preached about. But because you've shown me the truth in God's Word, I know I'll be changed."

Now I am not just sharing my opinion. I am showing you what it says in God's Word.

I am a covenant man, because of Jesus.

You are a covenant man, because of Jesus.

We are a covenant people, because of Jesus.

So, we aren't to look at each other by the flesh anymore.

Don't let that devil of prejudice and racism come into your house. Get him out of there. If you have problems with a black man or with a white man, it's time the two of you come together over communion and swear your allegiance to one another.

"But, preacher, you know how white folks are."

Don't stereotype. One bad apple doesn't spoil the whole bunch.

Yes, there are some crazy white folks. And there are some crazy black folks, some crazy Mexicans, some crazy Indians and some crazy Orientals. But when we get in Christ, we become one together.

Now I live in one of the most racist areas in the world: Atlanta, Georgia — the capital of the Civil Rights Movement. When I preach this message there, people don't like it. But I don't care. We now have folks of different ethnic groups who are ready and willing to come together. They know that is where reconciliation will occur.

I want to share a poem written by one of my personal aides in our church. It goes like this:

I am a black man, proud and strong.
But does that make the white and other races wrong?

Can I look at your skin and see what is deep inside?
Does the color of my skin give me authority to walk with pride?

Why is racism something not taught, but learned?
Why does the color of my skin make respect so hard to earn?

Why does our color make us speak with a different tongue,
Or make a difference in the way certain things are done?

Why does the color of our skin make some to become mad,
Or an interracial marriage make a happy family sad?

To be prejudiced against one another, we have no reason.
You are just another color as the change of the season.

Even though our color has a difference, are we not the same?
Or do we have enough courage to put God in blame?

For He said, "We are all created equally and come together as
    one."
So let's put our hearts together and let His will be done.

The skin we wear identifies one race from another,
But whatever your race may be, you are still my brother.

Amen.

CHAPTER 7

RECONCILIATION UNDER FIRE!

Racism, divorce, family feuds, arguments between friends and associates — all of these are devices the devil uses to hinder the ministry of reconciliation.

These are spiritual problems, which is why they cannot be solved politically with programs. They are the designs of the devil. He knows the end is coming, so he is trying to continually cause separation and division within the Body of Christ. He wants Christians to find some reason to dislike one another, so he uses forces like envy and jealousy and strife to keep some gap between us.

THE LOVE OF CHRIST IS THE KEY

Second Corinthians 5:14 says:

For the love of Christ constraineth us....

Verse 14 AMP says:

For the love of Christ controls and urges and impels us....

This is what the love of Christ does: it urges us; it controls us; it impels us.

Now, let's read the entire verse of Second Corinthians 5:14 KJV. It says:

For the love of Christ constraineth us; because we thus judge, that if one died for all, then were all dead.

This is a key statement. Again, verse 14 AMP says:

For the love of Christ controls and urges and impels us, because we are of the opinion and conviction that [if] One died for all, then all died.

Jesus is the One Who died for every human being on the face of this earth — for every black man, every white man, every Mexican man, every Oriental man. He died for *every* man, for *every* woman, for *every* boy and *every* girl. He died for our enemies and for our friends. So, as the Bible says here in verse 14, if One (Christ) died for us all, then we all are dead.

LOOK BEYOND THE FLESH

Second Corinthians 5:15 KJV says:

And that he died for all, that they which live should not henceforth live unto themselves, but unto him which died for them, and rose again.

Verse 15 AMP reads:

And He died for all, so that all those who live might live no longer to and for themselves, but to and for Him Who died and was raised again for their sake.

Jesus is saying, "I died for all of you; and since I died for you, all of you died with Me. Now once I live, you all can live, too."

Second Corinthians 5:16 KJV says:

Wherefore henceforth know we no man after the flesh: yea, though we have known Christ after the flesh, yet now henceforth know we him no more.

Verse 16 AMP says:

Consequently, from now on we estimate and regard no one from a [purely] human point of view [in terms of natural standards of value]. [No] even though we once did estimate Christ from a human viewpoint and as a man, yet now [we have such knowledge of Him that] we know Him no longer [in terms of the flesh].

Jesus is saying, "Since I died and you died with Me, now that we live, we don't live knowing men after the flesh." Do you understand what this means?

As a black man, I no longer see a white man in terms of the flesh — as a white man. I see him in terms of the Spirit — a fellow believer in Jesus Christ.

I don't see a man who once was a murderer in terms of the flesh. I see him in terms of the Spirit, as one who now has accepted Jesus as Lord and Savior of his life.

I don't look at a woman who once was a prostitute in terms of the flesh. I now see her through the Spirit, washed clean by the blood of Jesus.

How can we do that?

Because Jesus died for all of us and all of us are dead in Him. Now that we live in Him, we are not to look at one another in the flesh anymore. We died in the flesh so that we could live in the Spirit.

Don't look at me through my flesh because, if you do, you will always find something wrong. As believers in Jesus, you are dead and I died with you. When we got born again, we came alive in Him. Because of that, we don't see things the way we used to see them.

But what should we do when things happen that we don't like?

THE COLOR OF LOVE

DIE TO THE FLESH

We still want to respond the way we did when we were living in the flesh. We have a hard time forgiving because we had a hard time doing it in the flesh. We don't see how we can totally renew a relationship after we have been hurt by it.

Do you know why you can't do it? I will tell you.

You are supposed to be dead to the flesh and not see anyone else after the flesh. But you will never be able to do it until you die completely to the flesh and are able to live and see things through the Spirit. You have to trust God by faith and say, "If I do this by the Spirit, I believe God will honor me and do what needs to be done."

Let's look again at Second Corinthians 5:16 AMP:

Consequently, from now on (since we all are dead in Christ) *we estimate and regard no one from a [purely] human point of view [in terms of natural standards of value]. [No] even though we once did estimate Christ from a human viewpoint and as a man, yet now [we have such knowledge of Him that] we know Him no longer [in terms of the flesh].*

RECONCILIATION BETWEEN GOD AND MAN

Now, we must take all this into consideration: the fact that Jesus died for us, that we died together with Him and now live in Him, that we are to no longer see other believers and judge them by natural value only. Second Corinthians 5:17 from the *King James Version* says:

Therefore if any man be in Christ (the Anointed One), *he is a new creature: old things are passed away; behold, all things are become new.*

What just happened here? Reconciliation.

100

Verse 17 AMP says:

*Therefore if any person is [ingrafted] in Christ (the Messiah)
he is a new creation (a new creature altogether); the old
[previous moral and spiritual condition] has passed away.
Behold, the fresh and new has come!*

You know, you have to believe this by faith. After you get born again, and then wake up the next morning, this verse says you are fresh and new. God made you fresh and new for a reason.

Then Second Corinthians 5:18 KJV begins with these words:

And all things are of God....

God knows what we are thinking. So, don't be sitting there, thinking, *How can this be so?* You didn't have anything to do with it. Don't worry about how you are going to do things. It isn't of you anyway. This verse says, **And all things are of God.**

Continuing in verse 18 KJV, it says:

*And all things are of God, who hath reconciled us to himself by
Jesus Christ....*

God has restored union and friendship with the believer. The walls of partition are no longer standing between God and man; they have been broken down.

God now says: "The differences and the quarrels have been settled. After the disagreement or the enmity, friendship has been renewed. I have restored you into union with Me. I now have mercy on you."

NOW WE ARE GIVEN
THE MINISTRY OF RECONCILIATION

Here is Second Corinthians 5:18 KJV in its entirety:

And all things are of God, who hath reconciled us to himself by

*Jesus Christ, and hath given to us the ministry of
reconciliation.*

God has reconciled us to Himself so that He could give us the
ministry of reconciliation.

He didn't give it to the politicians, to the president, to the governors
or to local concerned groups.

He has given the ministry of restoration and reconciliation to those
of us who have been reconciled, who are in Christ, who have been
made a new creation in Him. Old things have passed away.

We who are dead in Him now live with Him. We are not to see
things in the flesh anymore, weighing them by these natural, mortal
means. We died with Him and have risen with Him.

We are a new species of being that never existed before. We have
been reconciled and unified back together with God. We sit where He
sits and see the way He sees.

Based on this Scripture, we can see we have been called into the
ministry of reconciliation. God is saying, "I have done this to you.
Now you go and do it to somebody else."

Now let's read Second Corinthians 5:18 AMP:

*But all things are from God, Who through Jesus Christ
reconciled us to Himself [received us into favor, brought us into
harmony with Himself] and gave to us the ministry of
reconciliation [that by word and deed we might aim to bring
others into harmony with Him].*

God is saying: "I brought harmony between you and Me. Now
you can do with others as I have done with you: you can bring others
into harmony with Me."

NOW YOU QUIT HOLDING THOSE SINS
AGAINST OTHERS!

Second Corinthians 5:19 in the *King James Version* says:

To wit, that God was in Christ, reconciling the world unto himself, not imputing their trespasses unto them; and hath committed unto us the word of reconciliation.

Verse 19 AMP reads:

It was God [personally present] in Christ, reconciling and restoring the world to favor with Himself, not counting up and holding against [men] their trespasses [but cancelling them], and committing to us the message of reconciliation (of the restoration to favor).

God isn't holding people's sins against them. He isn't holding their past against them. He isn't holding their mistakes against them. And He isn't holding against them what they did to you or said about you just last week.

Now, you have to quit holding things against those people. Quit holding it against them for the awful things they have said or done, or for the awful past they or their ancestors have lived.

God is saying: "I am not holding any of that against them. I have cancelled their sins and have committed to you the message of reconciliation, the message of their restoration to favor."

He has committed His word of reconciliation to us, the believers.

The word of reconciliation can only be carried by those who have been reconciled: godly men and women.

Their word of reconciliation is this: "God loves you, no matter what you have done to Him; and I can love you, no matter what you did to me."

The problem is, God's people are trying to reconcile others to God when they don't even want to reconcile those people to themselves.

They say, "It's all right if they get saved — just as long as they leave me alone."

Does that sound familiar to you?

It's important for us to remember that the word of reconciliation doesn't work unless we are maintaining our reconciled position as a new creation and a new species of being through Jesus.

Second Corinthians 5:20 begins:

Now then we are ambassadors for Christ....

Somebody says, "I am an ambassador because I am saved."

No, you are an ambassador because you have taken on the ministry of reconciliation. When you see distressing things, you will want to get in and restore them at all cost. You are the repairer of the breach. (Isaiah 58:12.)

THE FORCE OF RECONCILIATION

It goes on in verses 20 and 21 of Second Corinthians 5:

Now then we are ambassadors for Christ, as though God did beseech you by us: we pray you in Christ's (the Anointed One's) *stead, be ye reconciled to God.*

For he (God) *hath made him* (Jesus) *to be sin for us, who knew no sin; that we might be made the righteousness of God in him.*

Now I want to show you the force of this ministry of reconciliation, which people seem to have a problem getting involved in. What happens when you start actually doing this?

You may be thinking, *How can I humanly do what we have just read about? You have no idea what those people did to me. I would be a fool if I did that.*

But I know what I am talking about, because I have been through this. I felt that I had been betrayed by another race, so there was a huge gap between us. The way I saw it, that other guy was at fault.

God kept telling me to go and reconcile with that person, but I kept saying: "I'm not going to reconcile a thing. I've already been hurt. I feel like I have been used and abused. Why should I have to go and fix it?"

This is what God said to me then:

"Because I called you to be the fixer. I called you to the ministry of reconciliation. If you will reconcile, I will show you My power; I will show you My healing; I will show you what I can do as a result of your reconciliation."

After several months of my failing to say anything to reconcile with that man, I called him on the phone. When I did that, I found out God had changed the man's heart. We reconciled the situation, and the problem was resolved.

The Bible says if somebody has offended you, you are to go to that person. (Matthew 18:15.)

You might say, "Why can't he come to me? I'm the one who is hurting."

Listen to me: Your hurts, your pains, your problems should mean nothing to you. But the pains, hurts and problems of others should mean everything to you, because they mean everything to God. So, you don't have to worry about taking on such things.

I know this message isn't milk; it's strong meat. So just hang on.

I will give you an example in the book of Acts where there was discrimination going on. You have to be careful how you do things, because if you cause a separation, you will be causing a problem. Let me show you what I mean.

DIVISION IN THE EARLY CHURCH

Leaders have to be careful not to create separation. They can't get into the pulpit and preach, "The white man did this," or "Those black people did that," or "That teenager did this." By doing such things, they are creating separation.

I want to show you what was going on in the Early Church. Something happened here that needed to be reconciled. Let's look in Acts, chapter 6:

And in those days, when the number of the disciples was multiplied, there arose a murmuring of the Grecians against the Hebrews, because their widows were neglected in the daily ministration.

Acts 6:1

What was the division?

The Grecians against the Hebrews.

One group of disciples was discriminating against another group. They were taking care of some people, but they weren't taking care of their widows. Now notice what happened here:

Then the twelve called the multitude of the disciples unto them, and said, It is not reason that we should leave the word of God, and serve tables.

Wherefore, brethren, look ye out among you seven men....

Acts 6:2,3

They were saying: "We need to reconcile and to restore this situation. Discrimination has taken place because separation is there;

we have paid more attention to one group than to the other. So we need to fix it."

They didn't just pick anybody, such as a politician, to go and fix their problem. Notice the first thing they did was to say: "Let's look out among us and find seven men." Here in Acts 6:3 is the description given of those men:

> *...seven men of honest report, full of the Holy Ghost and wisdom, whom we may appoint over this business.*

The ministry of reconciliation has been given to the new creation, the new creature. It has been given to the one who is honest, who is full of the Holy Ghost, who has wisdom. They are the ones to be appointed over the business.

Continuing with Acts 6, verses 4 and 5, it says:

> *But we will give ourselves continually to prayer, and to the ministry of the word.*

> *And the saying pleased the whole multitude: and they chose Stephen, a man full of faith and of the Holy Ghost....*

After listing Stephen and the other men chosen to fill these positions, it says:

> *Whom they set before the apostles: and when they had prayed, they laid their hands on them.*

> *And the word of God increased; and the number of the disciples multiplied in Jerusalem greatly...* (vv. 6,7).

Notice it says they didn't just multiply — they multiplied *greatly*.

RECONCILIATION BRINGS INCREASE

Reconciliation produces increase; division produces decrease. If there is division, if there is a gap in relationship, there will be decrease.

Consider marriage as an example. Until the problem between a husband and wife is reconciled, they will never be able to "increase greatly."

The devil will do everything he can to cause some type of separation and division in relationships. If he can do that, then increase cannot come forth.

So, what is the solution to decrease?

Reconciliation.

It will produce "great increase."

It will also affect our enemies. The greatest enemies to the Early Church were the priests. It goes on in Acts 6:7 to say:

...and a great company of the priests were obedient to the faith.

Notice this: their enemies took note of the ministry of reconciliation, and it affected them.

What do you think would happen if people in the world saw you going out to reconcile differences with others? It would change their lives.

In the midst of people trying to cause division and separation between blacks and whites, suppose you were to appear and say, "I apologize." What do you think would happen?

THE ANOINTING WILL BE THERE

When people truly see the ministry of reconciliation — when they see that the atmosphere of reconciliation is there, that the anointing for reconciliation is there — it will change them.

Do you think God would actually give you a ministry and not give you the anointing to carry out that ministry? If He has given you the ministry of reconciliation (and He has), don't you know He has also provided the anointing for you to operate in that ministry of reconciliation?

After enmity has gotten into a situation, any born-again believer who moves out to restore union or friendship will have the anointing to do it.

That's why it is important that, when we notice a division, we operate in our ministry to bring reconciliation; then the anointing will show up, and we will always win.

It is never to be just me, the minister, trying to fix something when it can't be fixed. We as God's people are to go out and do it; then God will change hearts. The anointing is available to bring reconciliation and restoration.

Do you understand what I am saying? The anointing is present when God's people operate in any ministry given from God, because any ministry coming from God is anointed. God does not give a ministry that is not anointed.

When we are doing what God has called us to do, we will get results. The Word of God is so anointed that it can bring itself to pass. In Isaiah 55:11 God says: **So shall my word be that goeth forth out of my mouth: it shall not return unto me void, but it shall accomplish that which I please, and it shall prosper in the thing whereto I sent it.**

Let's see now if we can do our best to settle this hard point about separation and division within the Body of Christ.

BE A TEAM PLAYER

The Bible says, **Seek ye first the kingdom of God** (Matthew 6:33). Don't be seeking your own kingdom first.

By seeking your own ministry, you won't be involved in the ministry of reconciliation; you will be involved in the ministry of self. All your motives will be wrong. You won't be a team player. You will only want to magnify your own self by always singing the solo. Magnifying your own ministry is just another way to cause separation.

There is something about a person who doesn't want to be a team player. Others who are a part of the team realize that player can't be trusted. They know the first chance he gets, he will be trying to branch off and do his own thing. He will be thinking: *I'm only a team player when my motives are being fulfilled; but if they get interrupted, I won't play anymore; I'll just take my ball and go home.*

What will be the result of his thinking this way?

By magnifying his kingdom, he will have caused a division between himself and the team.

In football, that player can't score without the tackles, guards and center moving in front of him and blocking for him. He had better not get them mad by making the mistake of saying something on an interview like, "I'm bad all by myself; I don't need anybody blocking for me." After making that kind of comment, when he starts the first play of the next game, he will say, "Okay, fellows, are you ready? 344. 348. Set. Hut!" But all those protectors on his team will just step aside, and let him get trampled by the defense. And it all started because of division.

After joining up with a body of believers, you can't be concerned about your own ministry; you have to be a team player in your church. By being a team player, you will learn how to gang-tackle first, and you will be helping out where you are needed.

Don't worry about doing what God has called you to do. Just play with the team. After a while, you will find yourself out in the middle of the field. It will be you against the other guy, and you will have to make a solo tackle.

Do you remember what happens when division gets involved? We read about it earlier in Matthew 24:10. They get offended. They betray you. They hate you.

So, be careful, because separation and division are devices of the devil.

We have to stand against the devil's devices. But how do we do that?

By recognizing what Jesus did on the cross.

He shed His blood for each of us, regardless of our color. When will we, the Body of Christ, be able to look beyond color and see the heart?

CHAPTER 8

RECONCILIATION — IN HONOR OF THE BLOOD

Now you might be saying: "Why should I accept this ministry of reconciliation? What if I want the gap to stay there between us? Maybe I don't want us to pull together. Maybe I'm satisfied with us being apart."

Then let me inject something else into this discussion about reconciliation: the blood of Jesus.

Let's look in Romans, chapter 5:

For when we were yet without strength, in due time Christ died for the ungodly.

For scarcely for a righteous man will one die: yet peradventure for a good man some would even dare to die.

But God commendeth his love toward us, in that, while we were yet sinners, Christ died for us.

Much more then, being now justified by his blood, we shall be saved from wrath through him.

Romans 5:6-9

The way I see it, Jesus had to shed His blood for me in order to reconcile me to God. Now He has given to me the ministry of reconciliation, the word of reconciliation.

I NOW ACT IN HONOR OF HIS BLOOD

Even if I don't like you, and my flesh doesn't want to do anything for you, I would be moved to do it in honor of the blood of Jesus that was shed for me. My honoring of that blood is honoring my God and honoring my Lord, Who shed His blood for me. As the Bible says, if you honor God, God will honor you. (1 Samuel 2:30.)

It will move heaven when what we are doing is in honor of His blood. As Scripture says, we overcome our enemy, Satan, with the blood of the Lamb and the word of our testimony. (Revelation 12:11.)

I love you, and because I love you, I preach the Gospel. You don't have to love me back because what I do, I do in honor of the blood. I honor His blood more than anything or anybody.

It is like a man in the military. Why does he stand there and take all the verbal abuse from his sergeant? Why does he go overseas and risk his life when called upon to do so? He does it in honor of his country. That feeling of respect for his country moves him to do what he wouldn't normally do. He is willing to give even his life in honor of his country.

ATONEMENT

For if, when we were enemies, we were reconciled to God by the death of his Son, much more, being reconciled, we shall be saved by his life.

And not only so, but we also joy in God through our Lord Jesus Christ, by whom we have now received the atonement.

Romans 5:10,11

The Greek word translated *atonement* is *katallage*, which means total change.[1]

---

[1]Marvin R. Vincent, D.D. *Word Studies in the New Testament.* (Peabody, MA: Hendrickson, n.d.), vol. 3, "The Epistles of Paul," pp. 61,62.

I can be hardheaded and bullheaded sometimes, thinking, *Why do I have to do this? Why is this necessary?* But once I have entered into a time of repentance, God has a way of answering me by saying, "In honor of My blood."

REMOVE THE WALLS!

I remember one time when God said to me: "You dishonor My blood. You dishonor everything I have done for you, everything I have provided for you, if you don't remove the walls that have been built between relationships."

You see, it doesn't make any difference how you feel or what you think should be done when it dishonors Him. I will show you how we once were long distance from God, but were brought near to Him by the blood of Jesus.

Let's look in Ephesians, chapter 2:

For by grace are ye saved through faith; and that not of yourselves: it is the gift of God:

Not of works, lest any man should boast.

For we are his workmanship, created in Christ Jesus unto good works, which God hath before ordained that we should walk in them.

Ephesians 2:8-10

God has commanded us to walk in these good works.

Wherefore remember, that ye being in time past Gentiles in the flesh, who are called Uncircumcision by that which is called the Circumcision in the flesh made by hands.

Ephesians 2:11

Do you see the division described here? One side is uncircumcision; the other is circumcision.

That at that time ye were without Christ, being aliens from the commonwealth of Israel, and strangers from the covenants of promise, having no hope, and without God in the world.

Ephesians 2:12

Let me refresh your memory as a believer in Jesus Christ. There was a time when you were living in sin. You were a stranger, one who was separated from God. You didn't know about the Word. You had no hope and were on your way to an eternal damnation.

You were living far from God. Your life was a good-for-nothing, dirty mess. You were hooked on some bad habits. Maybe you were a liar, a cheat, a fornicator, a prostitute. Or, maybe you thought you were doing okay. But without Jesus as Lord of your life, you were on your way straight to hell.

There are lots of born-again people who are still strangers to their covenant of promise. They may be regularly attending church, but they still don't know the Word.

What happens when you are a stranger with God? You have no hope. You are without God in the world. In other words, you don't have a blueprint. How can you build a house without a blueprint?

But now in Christ Jesus (the Anointed One) *ye who sometimes were far off are made nigh* (brought near) *by the blood of Christ* (the Anointed One).

For he is our peace, who hath made both one, and hath broken down the middle wall of partition between us;

Having abolished in his flesh the enmity, even the law of commandments contained in ordinances; for to make in himself of twain one new man, so making peace;

And that he might reconcile both unto God in one body by the cross, having slain the enmity thereby:

*And came and preached peace to you which were afar off, and
to them that were nigh.*

Ephesians 2:13-17

What Jesus did on the cross was for the purpose of bringing us
together. What He did on the cross was for all who have sinned. There
is no difference. No matter who you are, because of the cross, you
have been made righteous. If you believe Romans 3:23, which says,
For all have sinned, and come short of the glory of God, then
all can be made righteous through that cross; what He did, He did
for all.

THE GOSPEL OF PEACE

When your body is sick, it's the Gospel of peace at work when
somebody says to you, "By His stripes you are healed." (1 Peter 2:24.)

When you don't know how to pay your bills, it's the Gospel of
peace at work when somebody says to you, "But my God shall supply
all of your needs according to His riches in glory by Christ Jesus."
(Philippians 4:19.)

That is the peace which passes all natural, fleshly understanding.
(Philippians 4:7.)

But we who are alive died with Him Who died for us.

We are not to live in the flesh anymore; we are to live unto God.

We are not to see things the way we used to see them — in the
flesh; we must see them through the anointed Word of God.

Peace comes because we hear the Word of peace preached that
will reconcile us.

FELLOWCITIZENS WITH THE SAINTS

Speaking of Jesus, the Scripture says, He:

...came and preached peace to you which were afar off, and to them that were nigh.

For through him we both have access by one Spirit unto the Father.

Now therefore [now that peace has been preached] *ye are no more strangers and foreigners, but fellowcitizens with the saints and of the household of God.*

Ephesians 2:17-19

We are fellow citizens. That means we have all rights to everything that has been promised in the new society. It thrills me to know I am a fellow citizen.

..fellowcitizens with the saints, and of the household of God;

And are built upon the foundation of the apostles and prophets, Jesus Christ himself [the Anointed One] *being the chief corner stone;*

In whom all the building fitly framed together [not separated anymore, but fitly framed together] *groweth unto an holy temple in the Lord:*

In whom ye also are builded together for an habitation of God through the Spirit.

Ephesians 2:19-22

This is not just a building where the Holy Spirit dwells; He dwells in us individually, and He wants to dwell in us corporately as well. He wants all of us to come together and be reconciled to one another. Then the Holy Spirit can express Himself corporately like He does individually.

This is what He is saying: "In honor of the blood, I carry the Anointed Word of reconciliation. In honor of the blood, I do what My flesh makes it hard for me to do. Those who have hurt and destroyed Me, who have rumored about Me, who have dogged Me to no end, I forgive. Now I seek reconciliation with them."

Jesus set the example for us just before He gave His life on the cross. Beside Him hung two thieves. One of them reviled Him, but the other one said, "Lord, when You get to Your place, will You remember me?" Jesus said to him, "This day you will be with Me in paradise." (Luke 23:43.)

That man didn't do one thing to earn it; he didn't have time — he was dying. So don't tell me a person on his deathbed can't make it to heaven.

Jesus was saying: "I am ready to reconcile, to bring the favor and grace of God to you, to bring you closer to God."

In honor of the blood, we must pray for those who have wronged us in word or in deed.

In honor of the blood, we must forgive those who have shown prejudice and injustice towards us.

In honor of the blood, we must seek reconciliation now for wrongdoings of the present and of the past.

It's time for us to resolve things we know need to be resolved. They only hinder what God wants to do in us and through us.

CHAPTER 9

RECONCILIATION THROUGH MERCY

I want you to know the devil is doing everything he can all over the world to cause division and separation. He is trying to get big fights to brew up everywhere.

Let's make up our minds that we aren't going to let division and separation come into our homes, into our marriages and especially into our churches.

In a previous chapter, we looked at a passage from Second Corinthians, chapter 5. Now I want to consider another aspect of this Scripture.

Therefore if any man be in Christ, he is a new creature: old things are passed away; behold, all things are become new.

And all things are of God, who hath reconciled us to himself by Jesus Christ, and hath given to us the ministry of reconciliation;

To wit, that God was in Christ, reconciling the world unto himself, not imputing their trespasses unto them; and hath committed unto us the word of reconciliation.

Now then we are ambassadors for Christ, as though God did beseech you by us: we pray you in Christ's stead, be ye reconciled to God.

*For he hath made him to be sin for us, who knew no sin; that we
might be made the righteousness of God in him.*

2 Corinthians 5:17-21

We have defined the word *reconcile*. But there is one of its meanings
which we haven't put much emphasis on. To reconcile means to be
merciful. Let's deal with that now.

When we refer to the ministry of reconciliation, we are indeed
talking about a ministry of mercy. This is a ministry that is willing to
restore friendship, to restore unity, to restore that which has been
disrupted or estranged. I want to start off by adding some balance to
some of the things mentioned earlier in this study.

BORN IN THIS WORLD AS A SINNER

Because of the sin of Adam, the first man, we all were born into
this world as sinners. Jesus said to Nicodemus, **Except a man be born
again, he cannot see the kingdom of God** (John 3:3). He was not
referring here to a physical birth; He was talking about our being
born of the Spirit.

We should not think the same way Nicodemus did. In response to
Jesus' statement, Nicodemus said in verse 4, "How can I be born again,
as old as I am; do I have to go back into my mother's womb?"

Jesus answered him by saying, **Except a man be born of
water and of the Spirit, he cannot enter into the kingdom of
God** (John 3:5). Jesus was talking about being born of the Spirit. To
be a sinner, all you had to do was be born into this world.

Now notice this carefully: We think sinners are people who steal,
kill, curse and don't do what God's Word says. But these actions are
the fruit of sin, the results of being a sinner. Don't be surprised when
a sinner is not doing right. He is only doing what he is supposed to

do: he is sinning. The fact is, sinners sin. So, don't get upset because of that.

I want you to understand this: there was only one thing you had to do to be a sinner, and that was to be born into this world. At that moment, you were born into sin. I don't care how good you are or how many times you go to church. Good doesn't count without God.

BIG GAP FORMED BETWEEN GOD AND MAN

For you to get into right relationship with God and be reconciled to Him, a big gap had to be closed. This big gap occurred because Adam committed high treason against God.

You need to understand what it means to commit high treason. It would be like someone entrusting you with something valuable, and then you betrayed his trust. That's what Adam did towards God.

Adam was entrusted by God to be lord over the earth. God had crowned him with authority, but then he turned and gave that authority to God's enemy, Satan.

As a result, enmity and estrangement occurred between God and man, and their fellowship was broken. Then that big gap was formed between them.

JESUS BRIDGED THE GAP

Jesus became the plan to restore that fellowship between God and man. Jesus was born into the earth and shed His blood as a sacrifice for man's sin. Then He declared before all creation that the quarrel was over, that the differences were over, that the gap had been closed.

By doing that, Jesus was saying to mankind: "I am the bridge. If any man wants to go to the Father, He must go by Me. I am the Way, the Truth, the Life." (John 14:6.)

So God reconciled us to Himself through the shed blood of Jesus. That blood was the price He had to pay for our reconciliation.

I submit to you that reconciliation will never come without a price. It will always cost you something. For a husband and wife to be reconciled, somebody has to pay that price. They must be willing to say they were wrong even when they know they were right.

Reconciliation will never be easy unless you do it in the Spirit and with the anointing of the Holy Ghost. Jesus said, **For my yoke is easy, and my burden is light** (Matthew 11:30).

Now listen carefully. We have been given this ministry to let people know that everything is all right, that God isn't mad at them anymore.

Let's look at Isaiah 54:5,6:

For thy Maker is thine husband; the Lord of hosts is his name; and thy Redeemer the Holy One of Israel; The God of the whole earth shall he be called.

For the Lord hath called thee as a woman forsaken and grieved in spirit, and a wife of youth, when thou wast refused, saith thy God.

Notice this is referring to us, the believers, as the Bride of Christ.

In verses 7 and 8 it says:

For a small moment have I forsaken thee; but with great mercies will I gather thee.

In a little wrath [or anger] *I hid my face from thee for a moment; but with everlasting kindness will I have mercy on thee, saith the Lord thy Redeemer.*

God says in verse 8, **with everlasting kindness will I have mercy on thee**. The word *kindness* here does not really express what this means. There is a verse of Scripture in the New Testament which says this:

> *And to know the love of Christ, which passeth knowledge, that ye might be filled with all the fulness of God.*

Ephesians 3:19

We are **to know the love of Christ, which passeth knowledge**. How can we know the love of God if it is impossible to know His love? How can we know love that passes knowledge?

GOD'S LOVE IS FULL OF MERCY

There are certain things you will never know until you get involved in them. You can read books about marriage and never really know how good marriage can be until you have experienced it for yourself. Do you understand what I am saying?

So, the only way we can really begin to understand the love of God is for us to get involved in it. We have to be reconciled to God, recognizing that war no longer exists between God and man. Jesus has come and bridged that gap.

The Greek word for love, which you may be familiar with, is *agape*[1]; the Hebrew word is *hesed*[2]. This is God's tender loving-kindness in hot pursuit of us. He is trying to make us aware of His presence around us and doing all He can to run over us with His blessings. That is kindness. Tender loving-kindness. The mercies of God.

---

[1]W. E. Vine, Merrill F. Unger, William White, Jr. *Vine's Complete Expository Dictionary of Old and New Testament Words.* (Nashville: Thomas Nelson, 1985), p. 382.

[2]Ibid., p. 142.

God is saying, **with everlasting kindness** (with *hesed/agape*) **will I have mercy on thee**. In other words, He will give us mercy.

When is it that we beg for mercy most of the time? When we know we really don't deserve it. When we have nothing left to fall back on. When we are guilty as charged. That's when we feel doomed, damned, disgraced.

But Jesus, with His precious love, saved us by His grace. We pleaded with Him, "Jesus, save me!" That's when He dropped the charges against us and dismissed the case.

Realize this: God has had mercy on you, and the charges against you have been dropped.

Maybe you remember the conversation between Elisabeth and Mary in the first chapter of Luke's gospel. Elisabeth was in her old age and had been barren, but she was now pregnant with John; her young cousin, Mary, a virgin, was to give birth to Jesus, the Son of God. They both gave glory to God, saying, "The Lord has had mercy on us!"

This is what a believer says sometimes when he has been blessed and knows he didn't deserve it. Maybe God healed his body or paid his bills. So, he goes to church and says, "Look, the Lord has had mercy on me. I have been reconciled with God. We are no longer enemies; we are now friends."

The word *friend* is a covenant word. The friendship between God and man has been restored by the blood of the Lamb.

GOD IS NOT MAD AT YOU!

You need to realize God is not mad at you. If that's what you have heard, somebody lied to you.

Maybe somebody told you that God gave you cancer because you didn't live right, or that your car was stolen because of the sin you had just committed, or that your family life is no good because you aren't praying right.

Maybe they told you in the hospital that you had a low blood count because of the way you acted toward your mama when you were growing up.

Maybe they told you the reason your children are on drugs is because of the mistakes you had made when you were raising them.

These kinds of accusations would make you feel that God is punishing you for what you did. But that's a lie!

God is not angry with you. He isn't punishing you by making you sick as a way to get back at you for what you did in the past.

God doesn't want to make you sick; He wants to make you well. He is the Healer, and by Jesus' stripes you are healed. He isn't giving you cancer; He can't — He doesn't have any cancer to give you.

Do you think God gets a kick out of seeing you hurt, or broke, or depressed, or lonely and on the verge of committing suicide because you don't think anybody cares about you?

That makes Him sound like an angry God. But He says His anger was for a moment. That moment has come and gone. Again, Isaiah 54:7 says:

For a small moment have I forsaken thee; but with great mercies will I gather thee.

This is good news. Aren't you glad to hear it?

MERCY OUTLASTS SIN

Now look at Isaiah 54:9:

For this is as the waters of Noah unto me: for as I have sworn that the waters of Noah should no more go over the earth; so have I sworn that I would not be wroth with thee, nor rebuke thee.

God is saying, "I swore it. Now I have reconciled thee."

Isaiah 54:10 says:

For the mountains shall depart, and the hills be removed; but my kindness (hesed/agape — my tender loving-kindness in hot pursuit) *shall not depart from thee....*

You may depart from Him, but He will not depart from you. Scripture says, **Surely goodness and mercy shall follow me all the days of my life** (Psalm 23:6).

God is saying: "The mountains shall depart and the hills shall be removed, but My tender loving-kindness and mercy shall not depart from you. In fact, My goodness and My mercy will follow you all the days of your life."

You might say, "Well, He won't follow me if I mess up."

Yes, He will. He made you a promise, and God does not lie. (Titus 1:2.) He said, "I will never leave you or depart from you." (Hebrews 13:5.)

You may go out and smoke some reefer, but God will still be with you. Why? Because He says He will never leave you. In fact, He says His mercy endures forever. (Psalm 106:1.)

What does this mean?

That His mercy will outlast all of your sin. His mercy has endurance, and He will follow you.

You can just keep acting like a fool, but He will be right there. He won't depart, and you can't get rid of Him. When you finally get it together, it will be because He never left you.

Listen, believer, do you want to win your unbelieving mate? The one you are married to may act as crazy as an old hound dog, but you have to keep loving him (or her). The Bible says love covers a multitude of sins and mercy endures forever. (1 Peter 4:8; Psalm 106:1.)

God is saying, "I promise that I won't depart from you." He is showing you that when He reconciles, He means the past is over with. His reconciliation isn't based on what you and I might do; it is based on what He has already done. God's love for you is not based on what you have done to be loved; He has already decided, "I love you, whether you want My love or not."

THE COVENANT OF PEACE

Continuing in Isaiah 54:10:

...my kindness shall not depart from thee, neither shall the covenant of my peace be removed, saith the Lord that hath mercy on thee.

What happens when reconciliation takes place? Peace comes. The confusion is over. The quarrel is over.

God is saying that the reconciliation has made you a partaker of the covenant of peace. It will bring security in the midst of turmoil to know that everything is all right between you and God. Once you know that, then you will know everything else will be all right, too.

You can say to the devil: "You had better leave me alone because God loves me. I'm not just His acquaintance; I'm His friend. I know Him by His name. We hang out all the time. He's so close to me that He said He would never leave me nor forsake me. He loves me so much that He knows the number of hairs on my head."

You see, God and I experience ecstasy because we hang out with one another. He is my Friend. There is that covenant word: friend — not associate or acquaintance, but friend. I am in friendship with God. We are in covenant together.

As a friend of God, I have a right to enter into the covenant of peace, the peace that passes all understanding.

In the natural realm, you should not be able to have peace. Before you got born again, you would have gone nuts. But now through Jesus you can have the peace that passes all understanding. You might not understand why you can have it; you just know that the Word in you has delivered peace unto you. Isaiah 26:3 says: **Thou wilt keep him in perfect peace, whose mind is stayed on thee: because he trusteth in thee.**

Reconciliation now means that I am reconciled with God, and He lets me know that everything is all right. I can say to Him, "There is peace between me and Thee."

Do you remember the announcement that was made by the angel at the birth of Jesus? He said, **Glory to God in the highest, and on earth peace, good will toward men** (Luke 2:14). The peace sacrifice had been brought to earth. The blood price was about to be paid. The gap between God and man would soon be closed.

Let's go on with God's words in Isaiah 54:10-12:

...neither shall the covenant of my peace be removed, saith the Lord that hath mercy on thee.

O thou afflicted, tossed with tempest, and not comforted, behold, I will lay thy stones with fair colours, and lay thy foundations with sapphires.

And I will make thy windows of agates, and thy gates of carbuncles, and all thy borders of pleasant stones.

Notice verse 11. The Lord is speaking here to all who are **afflicted, tossed with tempest, and not comforted**. He gives another reason why you ought to be comforted: God is not mad at you.

In John 10:10 Jesus said: **The thief cometh not, but for to steal, and to kill, and to destroy: I am come that they might have life, and that they might have it more abundantly.** I don't care which translation you read this from, Jesus was saying that God is not a killer. He is a lover, not a fighter — not yet anyway.

A PROMISE OF PEACE

Isaiah 54:13 says:

And all thy children shall be taught of the Lord; and great shall be the peace of thy children.

Why will your children be able to have peace? Because you have taught them the Word.

This is what you should declare: "Great shall be the peace of my children."

When the devil says to you, "Your child is using drugs again," you can say by faith, "No, great is the peace of my children. They have been taught of the Lord."

He may say in response, "Well, your kids certainly haven't been acting like it lately."

But you just stand firm and say: "Devil, I believe I have put enough of God's Word into those kids to yank them out of that situation. God isn't angry at me or at my child. The mercy of God hovers over my child. So, hear me, devil: great is the peace of my child! God is not mad at me, and He won't do something to my child to get back at me. So, get out of here, devil!"

If something happens to your children, quit blaming yourself. Did you do what you were supposed to do? If so, it isn't your fault.

Your child is a free moral agent. He can make up his own mind. After a certain age, he can do whatever he wants to do, and he won't be listening to anybody. So, you have to pray and declare that great is the peace of your children.

Scripture says, **Train up a child in the way he should go: and when he is old, he will not depart from it** (Proverbs 22:6). They might wander away for a while, but keep believing God's Word, and they will come back.

ESTABLISHED IN RIGHTEOUSNESS

Isaiah 54:14 says:

In righteousness shalt thou be established: thou shalt be far from oppression; for thou shalt not fear: and from terror; for it shall not come near thee.

When you are established in righteousness, you will be far from *what?*

Oppression.

What, then, is the assumption here? That when you are not established in righteousness, there will be an open door for oppression to come right on in.

When will you not fear and be far from terror? When you are established in righteousness.

Fear and terror **shall not come near thee**. Why? Because God said: "I am not mad anymore. If you will settle yourself in what I have reconciled between us, fear shall not come your way; terror and oppression shall not come near you. So, establish yourself in what I have reconciled unto you."

OPPRESSION IS NOT FROM GOD

Isaiah 54:15 says:

Behold, they shall surely gather together, but not by me....

Who shall gather together? Fear, terror and oppression, as had been mentioned in verse 14.

I know people lied to you and said that God is making you oppressed and full of fear. But look again at what He says in verse 15:

Behold, they shall surely gather together, but not by me....

I like this. God is saying, "You have been blaming Me for it, but I didn't have anything to do with it."

SEE BEYOND YOUR ENEMY
AND STAY IN LOVE

Isaiah 54:16 says:

Behold, I have created the smith that bloweth the coals in the fire....

In other words, God is saying: "It's true that I created the smith that blows the coals in the fire — old Lucifer, your enemy. I created him, and I can handle him. Reconciliation is still solid; it is complete."

Now let's go on in verse 16:

Behold, I have created the smith that bloweth the coals in the fire, and that bringeth forth an instrument for his work; and I have created the waster to destroy.

God did not create Lucifer for the purpose of destruction; He originally created him as head over praise and worship in heaven. But Lucifer chose to exalt himself by being like the Most High. He led a third of the angels in revolt against God and, as a result, was thrown out of heaven. (Ezekiel 28:12-15; Isaiah 14:12-15; Revelation 12:7-9.)

Now notice what God has said in this passage of Scripture. If you will receive reconciliation — if you will cross the bridge and close the gap, if you will by faith establish yourself in righteousness — then verse 17 will take place in your life:

> *No weapon that is formed against thee shall prosper* [in other words, be in control of you, of your circumstances or of your situation]; *and every tongue that shall rise against thee in judgment thou shalt condemn. This is the heritage* (inheritance) *of the servants of the Lord, and their righteousness is of me, saith the Lord.*

Now I hope you catch what I am about to share.

This verse says: **every tongue that shall rise against thee in judgment thou shalt condemn.**

For quite some time I had thought this basically meant we would be able to speak a word and condemn every person who talks about us. But I don't believe that anymore because of this study of reconciliation.

You see, God is telling us to walk in love and reconciliation. If I am walking in condemnation towards other people who have talked about me, that doesn't make me any better than them.

When a tongue rises up against you — when oppression or terror or fear rises up — you can condemn it. But you have to recognize that those are the weapons Satan uses against you to try to stop you. The people involved are not your problem. They have just opened themselves, either wittingly or unwittingly, to be used by the devil. Do you see what I mean?

GOD SAYS, "THE WAR IS OVER!"

Now let's continue in Isaiah, chapter 55:

Ho, every one that thirsteth, come ye to the waters, and he that hath no money; come ye, buy, and eat; yea, come, buy wine and milk without money and without price.

Wherefore do ye spend money for that which is not bread? and your labour for that which satisfieth not? hearken diligently unto me, and eat ye that which is good, and let your soul delight itself in fatness.

Isaiah 55:1,2

The Lord is saying: "The war is over, so sit down, eat and enjoy, for I have prepared the table and it is feast time. We are no longer fighting. I have reconciled you unto Me."

Incline your ear, and come unto me: hear, and your soul shall live; and I will make an everlasting covenant with you, even the sure mercies of David.

Behold, I have given him for a witness to the people, a leader and commander to the people.

Behold, thou shalt call a nation that thou knowest not, and nations that knew not thee shall run unto thee because of the Lord thy God, and for the Holy One of Israel; for he hath glorified thee.

Seek ye the Lord while he may be found, call ye upon him while he is near.

Isaiah 55:3-6

God is talking about reconciliation. He is saying: "Forsake your ways. The bridge has been built. The way has been made. Return unto the Lord. Come on home."

Verse 7 says:

Let the wicked forsake his way, and the unrighteous man his thoughts: and let him return unto the Lord, and he will have mercy upon him; and to our God, for he will abundantly pardon.

You have to forsake your thoughts. Those thoughts will keep telling you that it isn't right, that God is still mad at you. But He is not.

Yes, you were guilty. But as a child of God, you have been brought before the board of paroles. You have been pardoned. Your case has been dismissed. It's over. You have been reconciled. Now everything is all right.

GOD'S WORD IS THE KEY

Are you trying to figure out how this can be so? You might wonder, "Lord, I don't understand. How can You do this? How can You forgive me after the things I have done?"

He explains it in the next two verses:

For my thoughts are not your thoughts, neither are your ways my ways, saith the Lord.

For as the heavens are higher than the earth, so are my ways higher than your ways, and my thoughts than your thoughts.

Isaiah 55:8,9

It seems like a dilemma, but God is getting ready to show us how we can understand His thoughts and His ways. He says: "Right now in the position you are in — by refusing to receive My pardon and to operate in reconciliation — My thoughts and My ways will always be higher than yours."

Now look at verses 10 and 11:

For as the rain cometh down, and the snow from heaven, and returneth not thither, but watereth the earth, and maketh it bring forth and bud, that it may give seed to the sower, and bread to the eater:

So shall my word be that goeth forth out of my mouth: it shall not return unto me void, but it shall accomplish that which I please, and it shall prosper in the thing whereto I sent it.

God is saying: "My thoughts are higher than your thoughts; My ways are higher than your ways. But I have given you My Word. If you will receive My Word, you will be able to have My thoughts and understand My ways."

In the New Testament, it says, **We have the mind of Christ** (1 Corinthians 2:16). How do we have the mind of Christ? We learn His thoughts and His ways by getting His Word down inside us. We receive all God has through His Word.

God is saying: "My Word shall not return unto Me void, but it shall accomplish that which I please. That Word shall prosper by being in control of the circumstances and situations which I sent it to dominate."

Notice what the Word says in Isaiah 55:12:

For ye shall go out with joy, and be led forth with peace....

How can I believe that it has been accomplished? Because He sent His Word.

How can I believe that I am healed? Because He sent His Word.

How can I believe that it is going to be all right? Because He sent His Word.

What do I have faith in? God's Word.

I don't have faith in what I can see. Neither do I have faith in what

I don't see. I have faith in God's Word. That is my only connection with Him, because He is higher than me.

The bridge was made between God and man, and it is described in John 1:1:

In the beginning was the Word, and the Word was with God, and the Word was God.

The bridge was needed between God and man, so God's Word became flesh. Then we, through that Word, were given a way back to the Father. Hallelujah!

It is through God's Word that we now can make contact with Him — in our prayers, in our confession, in our faith.

God's Word is filled with the anointing of God and is so anointed that it can bring itself to pass. The Word is full of God's power. Look at Hebrews 4:12:

For the word of God is quick, and powerful, and sharper than any twoedged sword, piercing even to the dividing asunder of soul and spirit, and of the joints and marrow, and is a discerner of the thoughts and intents of the heart.

God's Word is the only thing that can affect this natural world by penetrating into the spiritual world. It pulls from the spiritual world into this physical world, giving us as believers authority over the things of this world.

Do you know what God is saying about His Word? That it will work. That it will prosper and accomplish that which He sent it to do.

God did not just send us a bunch of words in a book we call "the Bible." That book is filled with words that come from the heart of God — words that are filled with God's faith, with God's anointing, with God's power. It is the anointed Word of God!

We have been reconciled by God's Word through the blood of Jesus, which declares that it is so. This is a legal contract. The price for reconciliation through His blood has been paid.

God is saying: "I am alert to watch over My Word to perform it. I cannot lie, for if I say it, I have to do it. So, if I speak it, it will come to pass. This covenant has come out of My mouth, and I will neither alter nor change it." (Jeremiah 1:12 AMP; Titus 1:2; Malachi 3:6.)

We have been reconciled through Jesus. But if we don't receive God's Word, we won't receive the bridge that brings us back into restoration and friendship and union with God. It is His Word which causes that union and restoration to take place.

But if you don't take hold of this truth, you will never benefit from it. That's why a decision is necessary.

SO, DECIDE TO RECEIVE

If you sit there all day long and don't make a decision to receive what Jesus has done for you, this will never become a reality in your life.

Without the decision, there will be no reality. Decision is the open door.

You have to decide to get saved. God can't make you do something you don't want to do, especially if you don't want to receive His Word. God's Word is the avenue by which we get to God.

THE LIGHT WILL SHINE!

Isaiah, chapter 60, shows us the power of reconciliation. It prophesies what we are going to be in the last days when we receive our reconciliation.

Arise [in other words, change your posture and your position], *shine; for thy light is come, and the glory of the Lord is risen upon thee.*

For, behold, the darkness shall cover the earth, and gross darkness the people....

Isaiah 60:1,2

Here is where we come in as believers. The Lord is saying darkness shall cover the earth. And, today, darkness is covering the earth. But He has reconciled us unto Himself through Jesus.

Look at verse 2 in its entirety:

For, behold, the darkness shall cover the earth, and gross darkness the people: but the Lord shall arise upon thee, and his glory shall be seen upon thee.

This is why it's so important that you know you have been reconciled with God. We see this point in verse 3:

And the Gentiles (sinners) *shall come to thy light....*

But we won't know this Light if we have not received the fact that we have been reconciled back to God. The reason we have to accept this ministry of reconciliation is because one day the Gentiles are going to come to the Light.

Verse 3 continues:

And the Gentiles (sinners) *shall come to thy light, and kings to the brightness of thy rising.*

I prophesy this to you:

There will come a time when people will start looking at the Church and will see that there is no division, no separation, no racism among us. They will come to us and ask, "How are you able to do this?"

There will come a time when you will hear the word of the Lord say: "Arise and shine, for the Light has come. The glory of the Lord is changing posture and position among you, and the kings (presidents, governors, mayors) shall run to you for help."

This has already happened in South Africa. Ray McCauley has one of the most integrated churches in the area. All of the people in that church are getting along, because they love one another. The government is trying to figure out how they are able to do it, so that it can be done in the rest of their country.

So, political leaders will be looking at the Church. They will come to us and say, "Things aren't working for us anymore. Help us. Tell us what to do."

For us to be able to do that, we have to be hooked up to our Source through His Word. Then we can give them the wisdom and understanding they will need.

CHAPTER 10

TRUE FELLOWSHIP

As we have learned in our study, to be reconciled is to be restored to union and friendship.

What if you know someone who is still living in darkness, who has never received Jesus as Lord and Savior of his life?

God does not want you to hook up with that darkness; He says there is no friendship with darkness. The day you got saved, by believing in Jesus as the sacrifice for your sins, a wall was formed between yourself and that unbeliever.

This is where the Great Commission comes in. Jesus commanded us, **Go ye into all the world, and preach the gospel to every creature** (Mark 16:15).

So, you would have to reconcile before you would be able to have true fellowship with that unbeliever. There can be no fellowship between light and darkness. But that doesn't mean you don't have communication.

WHAT IS FELLOWSHIP?

Fellowship comes from a Greek word *koinonia*[1]. For us to have fellowship with another person, we have to give to one another and then receive from one another.

---

[1]Strong, "Greek Dictionary of the New Testament," p. 42, #2842.

As Christians, who are in *koinonia* with one another, our fellowship must be based on the Word; then it will be good fellowship.

In *koinonia*, I give something to another believer and then receive something from him in return. I am not afraid to receive from him, because I know he is of God; and he is not afraid to receive from me, because he knows I am of God.

But when I am in communication with someone who is not of God, who has not accepted Jesus as Lord and Savior of his life, my *koinonia* will be limited. I can give to that person and make deposits in his life, but I have to be careful not to let him make deposits in me.

My objective would be for him to eventually become involved in my spiritual family by receiving Jesus as his Lord. Then I would be able to receive from him, because we would be of like precious faith.

I want you to understand that, as a Christian, you can't hang around a Buddhist and be able to have true fellowship. Why? Because there would be no common denominator between you.

So, *koinonia* is important. You have to recognize where another person is coming from spiritually before you make up your mind to receive from him and to allow him to make deposits in your heart.

BE CAREFUL OF FALSE HUMILITY

We have to be careful about what we listen to, so that we can stay balanced.

You know, balance is the key to life.

But the Bible says in Proverbs 11:1 that a false balance is an abomination to God; in other words, it would be disgusting to God.

It's important that we stay balanced when we make a statement such as this: "Even if God never does anything for me, I ought to love Him anyway."

Now, this is true, but wait a minute. We are talking about the God Who is always giving, Who is the Rewarder of those who diligently seek Him. That's what the Scripture says in Hebrews 11:6:

Without faith it is impossible to please him: for he that cometh to God must believe that he is, and that he is a rewarder of them that diligently seek him.

For us to settle it in our mind that we ought to just love God and never expect anything from Him is just a statement of false humility. It would be a slap in His face. Really, it is a lack of faith.

According to the Scripture, we must believe that God is the Rewarder of those who diligently seek Him. So, we are to expect a reward from God when we act on the Word. In fact, we are a people who have in us a capacity to move when we are motivated.

God knows that, and He enjoys motivating us. He enjoys saying, "If you do this, then I will do that." As He told Joshua, "If you will meditate on My Word day and night, then you will be prosperous and have good success." (Joshua 1:8.)

God is not the type that says, "You ought to just love Me anyway, even if I don't do anything for you." That's an untruth. Why? Because God is always in the process of doing things for His people. Hebrews 7:25 says Jesus ever liveth to make intercession for us.

It's just a cop-out to say, "Well, even if you never get healed, you ought to love God." If I don't get healed, something is wrong, but it's on my part. I can expect my God to move on my behalf when I am believing Him to do so.

Now maybe Buddhists or Muslims or followers of Reverend Moon don't expect their gods to move (and they would be right; their gods haven't moved in all these many years). But I am in covenant with God Almighty, and I expect my God to move and to do what He says in His Word.

If He said it, I believe it. I didn't say it; *He* did. *He* started it; I am just taking Him at His Word. And since He is the God Who cannot lie (Titus 1:2), I have a right to take Him at His Word.

I can't walk around in false humility, saying, "Well, it's all right that God doesn't heal." No, it isn't. Why? Because He said He would heal me.

The only thing between myself and my God is His Word. If His Word isn't good anymore, then our entire relationship is no good. But He has reconciled me to His Word. He has given me the right to expect results by acting on His Word. Hallelujah!

So, be careful about listening to people with this false humility. God's Word is awesome. The fact is, He has said it; that means you can receive it.

YOU CAN TAKE GOD AT HIS WORD!

There is only one way we can really know God: through His Word. John 1:1 says:

In the beginning was the Word, and the Word was with God, and the Word was God.

For God not to do His Word would be for Him to deny Himself.

Have you ever been told that it is all right for God's Word not to come to pass? If so, then you were told a lie. Scripture says heaven and earth shall pass away, but God's Word will *never* pass away. (Matthew 24:35.) God's Word *will* come to pass. Glory to God!

The Bible says that God is ever mindful of His covenant; that He hastens, or watches over, His Word to perform it; that He looks to and fro throughout the entire earth to find a people to whom He can show favor and produce His Word on their behalf. (Psalm 111:5; Jeremiah 1:12; 2 Chronicles 16:9.)

That means I have to look at everything in the light of God's Word, because His Word is all I have. My philosophy and my opinions don't amount to a hill of beans. God said it, I believe it and that settles it!

The truth is, God's Word is settled, whether I believe it or not. Why? Because God said it.

I don't have to wait to see if He is going to settle it; it is already settled. It doesn't have to be brought before Congress for them to vote it into law; it is already the Law. Everything God says from His mouth becomes law without any vote from man.

GOD'S LOVE CREATES LOVE IN US

In understanding God's Word, we have to go back and read again what He has said in Second Corinthians 5:14 about the love of Christ, the Anointed One:

For the love of Christ constraineth us; because we thus judge, that if one died for all, then were all dead.

This verse in *The Amplified Bible* says:

For the love of Christ controls and urges and impels us, because we are of the opinion and conviction that [if] One died for all, then all died.

I will never forget the time I was asked why I got saved. I said, "Because I didn't want to go to hell, and I don't like fire."

"Shame on you!" they said, "You should have gotten saved because you love God."

The fact is, I didn't even know God at that time. I loved my mama more than God. I just got saved because I didn't want to go to hell.

But then somebody took the time to tell me what Jesus did for me — that He suffered and died for me before I was even formed in the womb. I found out what the cross was all about. I thank God that Jesus was resurrected from the dead, but every Easter I celebrate that I have been resurrected, too. That's a reminder to me of all that Jesus did.

Second Corinthians 5:14 says the love of Christ controls us and impels us. The fact that I see what Jesus has done for me in His love causes me to do what I wouldn't normally do.

The love of Christ causes me to love you, even if you have dishonored me.

The love of Christ causes me to love you, whether you are black or white, regardless of your past or my past, or our ancestors' past.

His love impels me, controls me, urges me to forgive. In the natural I might want with all of my heart to hate you by holding the past against you. I might want to say it and taste it and see how it feels to strike back. But the love of God controls me, and the love of the Anointed One won't let me do it.

So, if you are not being urged or impelled or controlled by the love of God, and you find yourself saying or doing things that you know you shouldn't, you need to look back and see what Jesus has done for you. Then you will allow the love of God to impel you to fix whatever needs to be fixed.

JESUS REPRESENTS ALL OF US

Again, Second Corinthians 5:14 says:

For the love of God constraineth us; because we thus judge, that if one died for all, then were all dead.

Notice what He says here. The love of God controls us because we are of the opinion and conviction that "if one died for all, then all are dead." We know that the "One" being referred to in this verse is Jesus. When Jesus died, He represented all of us. He is now the Ambassador representing us, and we are to be ambassadors representing Him, because He died for all of us.

Now follow me very carefully. First of all, we have seen that Jesus represents all of us. He represents every black, every white, every Mexican, every Indian, every Oriental — every man, woman, boy and girl. Jesus died for all!

So, the Scriptures are saying if that One (Jesus) died for all, then we all — every one of us — are dead.

DEATH OF SELF

Now look at Second Corinthians 5:15:

And that he died for all, that they which live should not henceforth live unto themselves, but unto him which died for them, and rose again.

What kind of death are we to participate in? The death of self. We have to die to ourselves.

Jesus did the same thing, didn't He? The night He knew He would be going to the cross as the sacrifice for the sins of mankind, there was a great temptation for Him to refuse to cut that covenant. But He prayed for strength. (Matthew 26:36-46; Mark 14:32-42.)

When He died for all of us, we all died with Him. From that day forward, we no longer live unto ourselves; we live unto Him Who died for us.

But what does this mean? We need to bring it up to where we are today. "Dead" men don't concern themselves with worldly activities. If we are "dead," then we must find out what we are to live for.

CHANGE YOUR ITINERARY

You see, I used to live only for the black man, for soul power. I made statements like, "Let's get all those white people for what they did to us in the past!" But I don't live for that anymore; I died to it. That's no longer in my plan or a part of my activities. I now seek the plan of the One Who died for me on the cross and rose again.

Then there are others who stand for white supremacy. They say, "I'm gonna shave my head and go kill some of those black people!" But Jesus died for them, too. They can put aside their plan and seek Him. He will meet them where they are and fill their hearts with love.

It's time somebody was willing to face this issue. It has to be dealt with, but in the right way.

So first, you must realize you have to change your itinerary.

Let's look at Second Corinthians 5:15,16 in *The Amplified Bible*:

And He died for all, so that all those who live might live no longer to and for themselves, but to and for Him Who died and was raised again for their sake.

Consequently, from now on we estimate and regard no one from a [purely] human point of view [in terms of natural standards of value]....

So, this is saying that our natural standards and values have died with Christ.

"AFTER THE FLESH"

Verse 16 from the *King James Version* says:

Wherefore henceforth know we no man after the flesh....

How is it that we would typically know a man "after the flesh"? By looking at the color of his skin.

In our mind we would immediately categorize him with a stereotype. We would conclude whether we like him or dislike him based on the information we have computed, and we would determine whether he will be a part of our life by judging him "after the flesh."

But as this Scripture verse says, we don't know man after the flesh anymore.

Well, Lord, if we don't know man after the flesh anymore, how are we going to know one another now?

I want you to think about what you go through when you meet people. First appearance is awesome. You check out a person by the way he looks and how he cares for himself. Your senses take over, and you begin to communicate and see what you can learn from that individual.

If you aren't careful, when you first see that person, the stereotypical image will immediately come into your mind, especially if he is of another color.

Let's say a white man, who has just met a black man, merely assumes that the black man is the same as all other "people of his color." It is obvious, then, to the white man that the black man will know how to play basketball. The fact that the black man has never played basketball in his life is beside the point. The white man has weighed the situation strictly by the flesh. That would be a stereotype.

On the other hand, let's say a black man meets a white man and says to him, "I want you to teach me how to play golf." Weighing it strictly by the flesh, the black man just assumes that the white man knows about golf. Again, we would have a stereotype.

As it says in Second Corinthians 5:16, we are to know no man after the flesh. To whom is this verse speaking? Christians — those who have been born again, who have died and risen again with Christ Jesus.

So, as a Christian, we have a new way to live, and we must learn this new way. We are not to see and do and judge things the way we used to. To do that would be continuing to live "after the flesh."

THEY KNEW CHRIST AFTER THE FLESH

Second Corinthians 5:16 goes on to say:

...yea, though we have known Christ after the flesh....

I thought this was interesting. It is saying that they once did estimate Christ from a human viewpoint as a man. How did they "know Christ after the flesh"?

When they saw Jesus in the flesh, they saw a Jewish man. Why? Because it would have been illegal for Him to give bread to the Gentiles. He had no right to administer the bread unless He was a part of that clan or that tribe. Jesus belonged to the tribe of Judah, one of the twelve tribes of Israel. So then, we can conclude that Jesus was Jewish.

What about His skin color? I would imagine He had a dark tan. He couldn't help it. The skin color of any person who lived in the area where Jesus lived would have been affected by those strong rays from the sun.

But this Jesus Who will come back to earth again won't be the little Jew boy born in Bethlehem. The Bible says His hair will be white as snow, His eyes will be like fire and His feet like brass. (Revelation 1:14,15.)

We won't know what color He is, because we will no longer know Him after the flesh. His flesh will be changed. It will be glorified. It will be renovated. It will no longer be the way it was when He walked the earth all those many years ago.

"AFTER THE FLESH NO MORE!"

Second Corinthians 5:16 continues:

...yea, though we have known Christ after the flesh, yet now henceforth know we him no more.

Are you one of those who has a problem with skin color? If so, then I have news for you. Guess what's going to happen to your looks when you take on your new renovation? The Bible tells us that when we see Jesus, we will be like Him. (1 John 3:2.) In fact, as far as God is concerned, there are only two races on the earth: believers and unbelievers. That is the big picture.

It's interesting when He says we don't know Him after the flesh anymore. The second half of Second Corinthians 5:16 AMP says:

...even though we once did estimate Christ from a human viewpoint and as a man, yet now [we have such knowledge of Him that] we know Him no longer [in terms of the flesh].

Knowledge of an individual in Christ produces deliverance from the flesh.

When I know you, as a believer, and obtain more knowledge about who you are in Christ, our flesh doesn't matter anymore. The pure fact that you are in Christ means you are in me. Why? Because I am in Christ. If you are in Christ, then you and I are together in Him.

It's just like when a mother starts disciplining all her children and says: "I gave birth to all of you. You all came from the same place, and I'm not going to have you hating one another and talking ugly to one another."

I believe God is saying the same thing. We all came from the same place — whether Jew or Greek, whether black or white — it doesn't matter. He is the same God of all.

Take into consideration everything that has happened now. He said that we died because He died. Henceforth, we no longer know one another after the flesh. Nobody looks at Jesus in the flesh anymore.

INGRAFTED IN CHRIST, THE ANOINTED ONE

In verse 17 of Second Corinthians 5, we see the key to what this is saying:

Therefore if any man be in Christ [the Anointed One], *he is a new creature....*

This verse in *The Amplified Bible* says:

Therefore if any person is [ingrafted] in Christ (the Messiah) he is a new creation....

That means we can't say we are in the Anointed One and live a hypocritical life. To be ingrafted means we must be committed.

Looking again in verse 17 KJV, it says:

Therefore if any man be in Christ (the Anointed One), *he is a new creature....*

What is the condition required before we can be a new creature? We must be in the Anointed One.

This Scripture doesn't say, "If any man be in church on Wednesday...." Just attending church won't make us a new creature.

So, if any man be in the Anointed One, he is *what?* A new creature. When is he a new creature? When he is in Christ, or in the anointing. He becomes a new species of being that has never existed before.

Watch what this verse says next:

...old things are passed away; behold, all things are become new.

Somebody might say, "That's hard, Pastor. It's a struggle."

But Jesus said, **My yoke is easy, and my burden is light** (Matthew 11:30). That means the struggle is over. The battle has been fought; the war has been won. **For whatsoever is born of God overcometh the world: and this is the victory that overcometh the world, even our faith** (1 John 5:4).

LET GO OF THE PAST

Again, Jesus says, **Old things are passed away**. But some of us are still in the process of letting go of those old things. Do you know what we do? We see something passing from us, and we grab it, saying, "Oh, no, don't go now!" When we finally let go of that, we see something else leaving us, so we grab it and say, "Oh, no, not you!"

There is a danger of remembering old carnal things — of not letting go of your past or of your ancestors' past, of not letting go of the wickedness that causes hatred to stay in your heart. Some things you remember will produce hope and will benefit your life. But if you keep remembering other things and don't learn how to forget, that will only produce division.

Isaiah 43:18,19 says:

Remember ye not the former things, neither consider the things of old.

Behold, I will do a new thing....

What did the New Testament scripture say?

Old things are passed away; behold, all things are become new.

2 Corinthians 5:17

When will God do the new thing?

When we stop considering those old things.

Let me show you what the devil is trying to do now. If a black person continues to live his life considering all the struggles of the past — how he has been treated and how his ancestors were treated — then he will have dammed up within him the new thing God is trying to do. That new thing will never happen as long as he keeps holding onto the old. Understand that we can still learn from our past struggles, but let's make sure that hate and division from the past don't become our teachers.

Have you ever met a hippie from the seventies who has refused to change? If you were to see him today, he would still be the same. He hasn't made any progress; he is going around with the same attitudes towards life he had back then.

We are hoping for another opportunity, and God is saying so clearly, **Remember ye not the former things** (Isaiah 43:18). He is saying, "Don't consider those things of old."

If you start hanging onto victories to the point that you are living in those past victories and are not being motivated to go towards new victories, then it becomes dangerous.

I used to do that in high school. I lived by the victory of knowing we had played a good game the week before. Then after four weeks had gone by, I was still talking about "last week." After a while, nobody wanted to hear about it again; they wanted to know about new victories.

GOD WILL DO A NEW THING

Let's go on in Isaiah 43:19:

Behold, I will do a new thing; now it shall spring forth; shall ye not know it?...

Look at what God is saying. When will He do the new things? When we stop considering the old things.

What are you doing when you are considering the old things? You are spending time meditating on the past, instead of putting faith pressure on what could be happening in the future.

It's an attack of the devil to try to use the natural parts of our lives to prevent us from going forward — from glory to glory to glory.

God is saying, "When you stop considering the old, behold, I will do a new thing."

Continuing in Isaiah 43:19:

> *...now it shall spring forth; shall ye not know it? I will even make a way in the wilderness, and rivers in the desert.*

Yes, what happened in the past was bad; and because of that, a wilderness and a desert were created.

To black people I would say, maybe we weren't paid for the work our ancestors did; but God is saying, "I will take the responsibility to reconcile with you."

That's what He did with the children of Israel who built an entire city. They spent four hundred years in slavery and weren't paid a dime. Do you know what happened at the end? God told them to go and borrow money from their neighbors. (Exodus 11:2.)

What is God up to? He is getting ready to pay you. But He is going to do it His way, not your way.

I would say to my black brothers and sisters, your attitude ought to be like Abraham. You ought not want the government to pay you back because you are black. You ought to say, "No, I don't want payment from the government. I don't want to say that a man made me rich. I want God to pay me back."

Anytime you invest in the vision of another, you have set yourself up to be rewarded by Almighty God. This is a spiritual principle; and when you live by it, you can't lose. The government isn't going to pay you anyway; it is so much in debt that it can hardly pay for itself.

But God hasn't forgotten. He said to Israel: "What I am going to do is to make a river in the desert, and I am going to make a way through your wilderness." That is the Paymaster showing up and saying: "I have not forgotten about your work and labor of love, which you have shown for Me, but I will repay."

So, I put my trust in no man; I put my trust in God.

I KNOW WHO I AM!

My wife, concerned about my preaching this message, said to me: "Sweetheart, do you think people will accuse you of losing your identity and saying you have forgotten who you are?"

To a certain point, I have to agree. I am working hard to forget who I was and am trying to learn who I am. As I learn who I am, I find out I am "that."

You may be puzzled now and are wondering what I mean. I am identifying with the truth which has changed the facts of my life.

When I look in Scripture and see healing, I say, "I am *that*." When I see prosperity, I say, "I am *that*." When I see the Church being described as a holy generation, a royal priesthood, I say, "I am *that*." When I see those who have been called out of darkness into the marvelous Light to offer unto Him praise, I say, "I am *that*."

Regardless of how I used to be — regardless of how poor I was, regardless of my own prejudice and my own problems in life — I now have gotten involved with the truth of who I really am in Christ Jesus.

This truth has changed my past, and now I know who I am. I am blessed coming in and blessed going out. I am the head and not the tail. I am above and not beneath. I am always blessed, always prospering. I am the glorious production of God, the workmanship created in Christ Jesus unto good works. I died with Him, and I no longer look at others by the flesh. (Deuteronomy 28:6,13; Ephesians 2:10.)

THOSE OLD THINGS HAVE DIED

Let's look again at Second Corinthians 5:17:

Therefore if any man be in Christ, he is a new creature: old things are passed away; behold, all things are become new.

It says, **Old things are passed away**. You know, when somebody dies, we say they have "passed away." And that's what it means here in this verse — that those old things have died.

Then it says, **Behold, all things are become new.** When did "all things become new"? When those old things passed away. You see, the seed for new things is the death of old things.

Maybe you are trying to get new seeds in your finances. In order to see new things, there has to be a death in some area. You have to die to greed and to that habit of robbing from tithes and offerings. You have to die to self, because all of those old things are motivated by self.

GOD HAS RESTORED
HIS UNION WITH MAN

Second Corinthians 5:18 says:

And all things are of God, who hath reconciled us to himself by Jesus Christ, and hath given to us the ministry of reconciliation.

Through Jesus, God has restored the union that was between God and man in the Garden of Eden. You need to understand the division and separation which occurred at that time. What was divided? Sin and disobedience divided the presence of God from the man, Adam.

I want you to look at how man had wronged God, and continually remind yourself of what God could have done had He not been full of love.

In the beginning, God gave man all authority over the world, but man turned and gave that authority to God's enemy, Satan. Then Satan used that authority to kill God's Son, Jesus, by having Him hung on the cross.

God could have held that against all of mankind. Sitting there on His throne, He could have said, "I am not going to forgive them for their sins!"

But He didn't do that. He loved all of us — people of every race — enough to forgive us for the sinful act done against His Son.

GOD HAS CANCELLED OUR SINS!

Let's look at Second Corinthians 5, verse 19. I like this. It says:

To wit, that God was in Christ [in other words, God was personally in Christ], *reconciling the world unto himself, not imputing their trespasses unto them; and hath committed unto us the word of reconciliation.*

This verse in *The Amplified Bible* reads:

It was God [personally present] in Christ, reconciling and restoring the world to favor with Himself, not counting up and holding against [men] their trespasses [but cancelling them], and committing to us the message of reconciliation (of the restoration to favor).

God is not holding our sins against us. He has cancelled them. Glory to God. Isn't that wonderful?

IT'S TIME WE CANCELLED THEM, TOO!

Well, if God can cancel our sins, don't you think you and I should cancel them, too? Don't you think a white man and a black man should be able to face each other and cancel the hard feelings they have had toward one another, maybe all of their lives?

God is demonstrating to us what it was like for Him to forget the past and be willing to be reconciled with man. That's what man must be willing to do. As brothers and sisters in Christ, regardless of our racial differences, we must be reconciled with one another.

As a white person, you might say, "I will never like black people as long as I live, because it was a black man who killed my sister."

But I didn't do it — can you cancel it?

You might think all black people look alike. Just come a little closer, and you will see that we do look different.

The same is true with black people who think all whites look the same. I remember one time when I saw an elderly white woman, I thought, *My God, they all look alike when they get old*. But they really don't. I was weighing that by my flesh, and I had not gathered the knowledge to really know them.

Once you have gathered the knowledge to know an individual, then you will see that person as he really is, not as you had always thought he would be.

So, God has cancelled your sins. How about you cancelling some things against others, instead of continuing to hold onto them so tightly? Maybe that's why you can't get rid of your debt — because you won't let go of other things in your life.

I believe it's time for us to cancel some past experiences. We need to say, "Okay, it was done. I feel terrible that it happened and I didn't like it, but I will cancel it." That's what reconciliation is all about.

We may never get to the point where we can understand everything that has happened, but that's okay. It isn't always important that we understand every jot and tittle of what went on in the past.

"HUMBLE YOURSELF"

In Matthew 18:4 Jesus is really trying to demonstrate conversion, saying we must become like little children. I like what He says in this verse:

Whosoever therefore shall humble himself as this little child, the same is greatest in the kingdom of heaven.

It takes humility to walk in this ministry of reconciliation. When you humble yourself, you say, "God, regardless of what happens, I honor Your blood higher than anything, and I submit myself to Your Word."

Isn't it amazing how little children can play with one another, regardless of their skin color?

When my daughter went to the playground one day, she met a little white girl. They immediately became best friends. The little girl was always asking her mother to take her back there so she could play with our daughter.

My wife got upset one time when our little daughter saw a man and said, "What is that white man doing here?" My wife said: "Where did you learn that? He is a man, so don't be referring to him as a 'white' man. We want you to understand that, regardless of their color, they are people first. We will look at the skin color later."

That's what we do. We look at the fact that folks are people first. I don't believe a black dog would have a problem with a white dog. It would never say, "We can't mate because you're a white dog and I'm a black dog." No, a dog is a dog.

Well, what does the Bible say about marriages of whites and blacks? I will tell you exactly what the Bible says about it: absolutely nothing!

GOD SEES ONLY TWO RACES OF PEOPLE

Since we all have died and don't look at each other by the flesh anymore, do you know what the Bible says about marriage? It says: **Be ye not unequally yoked together with unbelievers** (2 Corinthians 6:14).

In the eyes of God, there are only two races: believers and unbelievers. That's all God sees. This means there is discrimination, but it isn't against people of another color; it is against unbelievers.

So God is concerned about believers fellowshipping or joining themselves with unbelievers. He is not nearly as concerned as man is with a black marrying a white, or a Mexican or Oriental marrying someone of another race. Our fellowship with other people should be based strictly on one criteria: whether they are brothers and sisters in Christ.

THE NEXT SUBJECT IN OUR STUDY

I want us to look now at the topic of living above carnality. The level of carnality is where the devil operates. So I want us to shine the light on him — not to give him any glory, but to let him know that we know where he is and how he operates.

CHAPTER 11

THE LEVEL OF CARNALITY

Let's begin in Romans, chapter 8:

There is therefore now no condemnation to them which are in Christ Jesus, who walk not after the flesh, but after the Spirit.

For the law of the Spirit of life in Christ Jesus hath made me free from the law of sin and death.

For what the law could not do, in that it was weak through the flesh, God sending his own Son in the likeness of sinful flesh, and for sin, condemned sin in the flesh:

That the righteousness of the law might be fulfilled in us, who walk not after the flesh, but after the Spirit.

For they that are after the flesh do mind the things of the flesh; but they that are after the Spirit the things of the Spirit.

For to be carnally minded is death; but to be spiritually minded is life and peace.

Because the carnal mind is enmity against God: for it is not subject to the law of God, neither indeed can be.

So then they that are in the flesh cannot please God.

But ye are not in the flesh, but in the Spirit, if so be that the Spirit of God dwell in you. Now if any man have not the Spirit of Christ, he is none of his.

Romans 8:1-9

Now let's define the word *carnal*. It means being from the flesh, or fleshly; being governed by human nature, instead of by the Spirit of God.[1]

After having studied this, I would define carnality as a form of living or thinking that excludes God's Word. It is being unspiritual.

Jesus said, **The words that I speak unto you, they are spirit, and they are life** (John 6:63). To be living spiritually is to be living by God's Word, because when you live by the Word, you are living by God's Spirit. So, if you have been born again, you have been delivered from the flesh.

Jesus has delivered us. He has given us His Word. He has given us His Spirit. He has given us His name. We don't have to yield to the flesh. If we operate like we are supposed to, our flesh will come under subjection to our spirit.

Either you are walking in the Word and by His Spirit, or you are walking in the flesh. You can't do both. When you cease doing the Word, you will begin walking in the flesh.

Romans 8:2,3 says:

For the law of the Spirit of life in Christ Jesus [the Anointed Word] *hath made me free from the law of sin and death.*

For what the law could not do, in that it was weak through the flesh, God sending his own Son in the likeness of sinful flesh, and for sin, condemned sin in the flesh.

Notice what this says. There was a situation that arose, separating God and man through sin, so God sent His Son, Jesus, as the solution. It says God sent His Son **in the likeness of sinful flesh** and He **condemned sin in the flesh.**

---

[1]Vine, p. 89.

Verse 4 tells why:

That the righteousness of the law might be fulfilled in us, who walk not after the flesh, but after the Spirit.

But there is a condition: these things happen for those **who walk not after the flesh, but after the Spirit.** So, we have been given a choice in life: we can live according to God's Word and by His Spirit, or we can live by the flesh. Now look at Romans 8:5:

For they that are after the flesh do mind the things of the flesh; but they that are after the Spirit the things of the Spirit.

If you are walking by the things of the flesh, then you will have those fleshly things on your mind. For you to walk in the Spirit, you have to mind the things of the Spirit.

SEPARATION FROM GOD

Romans 8:6 says:

For to be carnally minded is death....

What is this saying? That to be carnally minded is to be fleshly minded, to be thinking unspiritually, to be living without God's Word. That brings separation from God, and to be separated from God means death.

Any person who isn't born again is on a one-way street to death. When he dies physically, he will enter into eternal separation from God as a result of the sin of having rejected the Lord Jesus Christ.

Every time you, as a believer, choose to live in the flesh, you are causing a spirit of division to come between yourself and God, Who is your Source. That will affect everything in your life — your prayers, your giving, your confession — because living in the flesh separates you from the power of God.

LIFE AND PEACE

Romans 8:6 continues:

...but to be spiritually minded is life and peace.

Did you know life and peace go together? How do you get life and peace in your life? By being spiritually minded.

The life that is produced by being spiritually minded is the God-kind of life — the abundant life.

It was this life the rich young ruler wanted to obtain when he asked Jesus, **Good Master, what shall I do to inherit eternal life?** (Luke 18:18). What did Jesus tell him to do? To sell what he had and to give it to the poor. For him to have done what Jesus said would have produced that higher eternal life and peace. But notice his response: **When he heard this, he was very sorrowful: for he was very rich** (v. 23).

The peace that comes from being spiritually minded will bring security in the midst of a storm. No matter what storm you may be going through in your life, when you become spiritually minded, you will know security.

This security simply means if you won't think like the world, but instead will think like God's Word, you will feel safe, regardless of what happens around you.

By having the Word on your mind, there is nothing the devil can do to destroy that security. You will know the peace that passes all understanding. (Philippians 4:7.)

CARNALITY — THE ENEMY OF GOD

Romans 8:7 says:

The carnal mind is enmity against God....

In other words, operating in carnality is an enemy of God. Why is that?

Think about the heart of God. Why would operating in a carnal mind be an enemy to God? Because it takes us away from Him.

Carnality is not based on God's Word. It is against what God stands for. It prevents God from doing what He desires to do in our lives. Can we mix carnal things with spiritual things? No.

God is in heaven, saying: "I want to bless you, but I can't if you keep operating according to the world's system. As long as you behave carnally, you prevent Me from working on your behalf. But when you start operating spiritually, you will be where I can do what I want to do in you and through you."

If you are one of those who thinks you are doomed to die of cancer, God says, "I can't do anything for you. Your carnality is an enemy to My life."

If you are one who thinks you are supposed to be poor, God says, "I can't help you. You won't agree with My Word."

Again, Romans 8:7 says:

Because the carnal mind is enmity against God: for it is not subject to the law of God, neither indeed can be.

Living in carnality is not being subject to the law of God. Certain laws in the Word of God will never work for you if you are not agreeing with them.

You might say, "It takes faith to get the Word to come to pass." But your carnal mind keeps telling you, "It won't work!"

If you need to pay a bill, carnality says, "You had better hold on to all the money you have." Spirituality says, **Give, and it shall be given unto you** (Luke 6:38).

God's Word won't come to pass for the carnal mind, because carnality is not subject to faith or to the Word of God; carnality is subject only to the flesh.

Fleshly things won't make themselves subject to or respond to spiritual things. Those things of the flesh will always satisfy the senses. If by chance spiritual things begin to satisfy your senses, you had better reevaluate whether the "spiritual" things at work in your life really are spiritual.

Look at Romans 8:8:

So then they that are in the flesh [or walk in carnal ways]
cannot please God.

It's just this simple: those who are not living their lives by the Word cannot please God.

THERE IS A HIGHER REALM

Now look at Romans 8:11:

But if the Spirit of him that raised up Jesus from the dead
dwell in you, he that raised up Christ [the Anointed One]
from the dead shall also quicken your mortal bodies by his
Spirit that dwelleth in you.

This is Spirit power affecting mortal flesh. The realm of the Spirit is a higher level of existence than the natural realm we live in here on earth.

God is trying to move us into that higher spiritual realm. That's why He sent Jesus: to provide a way for us to enter into that realm, a super-realm which produces super-strength.

Can you see what's happening here? There is the carnal, or fleshly, level. Then there is the spiritual level, which is higher than the carnal level.

"BABES IN THE ANOINTING"

Now let's look at First Corinthians, chapter 3. In verse 1 the apostle Paul says:

And I, brethren, could not speak unto you as unto spiritual,
but as unto carnal, even as unto babes in Christ.

In other words, Paul is saying: "There are certain ones among you who aren't spiritual because of their flesh. They are only babes in the anointing."

Who are "babes in the anointing"? Those who are born again but are still being fed milk. They have not yet reached the place where they can accept the meat of God's Word. These spiritual babies can only suck milk and eat soft food; they have failed to develop the necessary tools to handle the strong meat.

Development and growth are two different things. We can grow, but to develop requires some pressure.

As an example, the body of a male can continue to grow until he is in his twenties. But for him to develop his body, he needs to spend time in the weight room, putting pressure on his muscles.

Look at verse 2 of First Corinthians 3:

I have fed you with milk, and not with meat: for hitherto ye
were not able to bear it, neither yet now are ye able.

I have found that a lot of people in the Church could be living under the anointing, but they are still sucking on the milk of God's Word. There are many things we ministers can't say to these spiritual babies, because they don't have the necessary tools to deal with the meat of God's Word.

Notice Paul refers to babes as those who are saved but are still subject to some carnality. As a pastor, I have to keep giving milk to many in my congregation because they are still subject to carnal things.

You see, a baby knows how to cry, and it often does, because its entire existence is based on the flesh. But as that baby begins to grow — as discipline is administered, as it learns and develops — it reaches the point where it doesn't need Pampers anymore. It is taught how to operate in the system.

The Bible says the meat of God's Word will affect our spirit to the point that we will be able to discern the difference between good and evil. (Hebrews 5:14.)

Spiritual babies are always subject to evil and to deception because they cannot discern between good and evil. The carnality still operating within them causes them to be offended. As long as they continue doing fleshly things that don't line up with the Word, their spiritual development will be hindered. It will be almost impossible for them to learn how to chew the strong meat of God's Word.

These spiritual babies don't like order. They don't like to hear people in church telling them what to do. They are still carnal. What they are able to receive is limited, because they don't have the necessary tools.

So what is the answer here? They have to grow up.

What is the sign of growth? Maybe you think it is the number of years you have been born again, but it isn't. The sign of true growth is obedience. You grow up spiritually by being willing to obey everything God tells you to do in His Word.

There may be times when you will read in the Bible where God says to do something, and you won't quite understand why you are to do it. You just have to be willing to do it anyway — simply out of obedience to God and His Word.

But there should come the time in your life when, instead of being offended by somebody who does something against you, you just walk away and refuse to receive that offense. When you reach that point, you will know then that you have grown up, that you have gotten off the milk of God's Word and have learned to eat the strong meat. Then you can just pat yourself on the back!

The implication of First Corinthians 3:2 is God telling you: "You have been given the milk and you have been fed; now you should be growing up."

As a parent, you have to go to the store and buy the formula to feed your baby. But after time goes by, that little one reaches the point where he is able to chew meat.

What happens, though, when baby Christians won't receive what Jesus has already done for them?

It is like Jesus has given them a ladder reaching into the spirit realm, but they keep knocking it down. They just don't want to leave this carnal realm.

Jesus keeps telling them He has presented a higher way of living. But they say, "I just can't see how that's going to work; it doesn't make sense." As long as they stay in that rut, they will never grow out of their carnality.

That's why you have to get your senses trained with spiritual meat, so that you can discern the difference between good and evil. Milk is good for a while, but you need to get some of God's meat into your system. Do you understand what I am saying?

The whole objective is for us to get out of the carnal realm. Why? For the sake of the anointing.

ENVY, STRIFE AND DIVISIONS

When spiritual babies still are not able or willing to grow, Paul gives a reason in First Corinthians 3:3 as to why that growth has not occurred. Notice verses 3 and 4:

*For ye are yet carnal: for whereas there is among you envying,
and strife, and divisions, are ye not carnal, and walk as men?*

*For while one saith, I am of Paul; and another, I am of
Apollos; are ye not carnal?*

For this kind of separation to occur within the Church means we
are still being carnal. We have not yet recognized that, regardless of
our denominational beliefs, we must be willing to come together in
the Body of Christ. That means we will not be able to receive strong
revelation on unity in the Body as long as we continue to look at our
differences.

You can't be going around, making comments like, "God only
uses the black man," or "God only uses the white man." That will
only keep you in this level of carnality, and you will be continually
acting in the flesh. God doesn't deal with the flesh; He deals with the
heart, or spirit, of man.

If you really want to get some results in your life, you have to step
beyond this level of carnality. But Satan will try his best to keep you
there. Let's take a look now at how he operates.

CHAPTER 12

THE DEVIL AND THIS CARNAL WORLD

Now let me show you the beginning of all the divisions in the earth, which we now see in the Body of Christ. You will be able to see more clearly where the devil stands in all of this.

SATAN WAS CONDEMNED
TO THE LEVEL OF CARNALITY

Genesis, chapter 3, is where the Serpent comes into the picture. By being very subtle, he uses deception to cause Adam and Eve to yield to sin. God speaks to him about that sin, and this is what He says in verse 14:

> *And the Lord God said unto the serpent, Because thou hast done this, thou art cursed above all cattle, and above every beast of the field; upon thy belly shalt thou go, and dust shalt thou eat all the days of thy life.*

I would say this curse sounds eternal and permanent. That is when the Serpent (Satan) was condemned to the level of carnality.

Dust is probably one of the closest things to operating carnally. How did God make man? Out of the dust of the ground. Isn't it interesting, then, that we are talking about living in the flesh? Flesh came out of the dust of the ground, and that is where the devil was forced to operate.

When God spoke the curse to the Serpent, He was saying to the devil: "I condemn you to operate in the realm of carnality, the realm of the flesh."

You need to understand that, before this, the devil was the anointed cherub, Lucifer, who had been given tremendous abilities as an archangel. But he was cast out of heaven. Now he is condemned to operate only in the area of the flesh — carnality. That's why carnality is such an enemy to God — because that's where Satan is being held in custody.

Now follow me carefully. I am telling you, we don't ever have to worry about the devil anymore.

Look at Isaiah 65:25:

The wolf and the lamb shall feed together, and the lion shall eat straw like the bullock: and dust shall be the serpent's meat.

We can understand the word *meat* here to mean "resources." It is similar to what is found in the book of Malachi when it talks about tithing. Malachi 3:10 says:

Bring ye all the tithes into the storehouse, that there may be meat (or resources) *in mine house.*

Now what is meant in Isaiah 65:25 when it says, **dust shall be the serpent's meat?** That the only resources the Serpent has available to him now are those which come from the natural realm, from the area of the flesh, from carnality.

The devil is limited to carnality. He is bound by the resources of the flesh. He works by using people's words and actions against one another, as well as things in this natural, fleshly realm, such as lust, lasciviousness, thoughts and suggestions.

THE DEVIL'S RELATIONSHIP
WITH CARNALITY

Now look at First John 3:8:

He that committeth sin is of the devil; for the devil sinneth
from the beginning....

This speaks of the devil's relationship with carnality, with the flesh.
It says he who commits sin is of the devil — of the carnal, of the flesh,
of the dust realm, because that's what the devil is.

Again, verse 8 says:

He that committeth sin is of the devil; for the devil sinneth
from the beginning. For this purpose the Son of God was
manifested....

Why was the Son of God manifested? It goes on in verse 8:

...that he might destroy the works of the devil.

Where can the works of the devil be found?

In the flesh.

Jesus was manifested to destroy the works of the devil. But I wonder
if we really understand what Jesus did in the flesh.

JESUS LOOSED MAN FROM SIN

The story we hear most often is how Jesus came down on our
level. And that's true; He did. He took on flesh and came in the form
of mankind to meet us at the point of our need. But He didn't stay on
our level. He didn't come here to stay. Glory to God!

Again, as First John 3:8 says, Jesus came **that he might destroy**
the works of the devil. The word *destroy* in the Greek is *luo*, which

means to loose[1], or to set free. Jesus didn't come to annihilate sin. Let me prove this to you.

Did you happen to see any sin during this past week? Of course, you did. Well, stop and think about it: if sin had been annihilated, you wouldn't see it anymore, would you?

So, Jesus came to loose us from that sin. We don't have to sin anymore. Jesus got the keys to sin, unlocked the handcuffs that kept man bound and flung open the jail doors for us.

Now Jesus has done what was necessary to loose you and make you free. But it's up to you: You have to obtain your liberation and walk in your liberty. If you want, you can put those cuffs back on your wrists and close those doors behind you.

Unfortunately, many Christians are being held captive, because they keep walking in the flesh.

God said in Deuteronomy 30:19:

I call heaven and earth to record this day against you, that I have set before you life and death, blessing and cursing: therefore choose life, that both thou and thy seed may live.

God was saying: "I have placed before you life and death, blessing and cursing. If you do not know what to choose, then I will give you a hint: choose life!"

So, God sent His Son, Jesus, to set us free from sin.

Now we hear much about being set free from sin, but I really think it goes deeper than that. Jesus came to set us free from a realm of the flesh, of the carnal, of the devil.

---

[1]Vine, p. 164.

MAN WAS CREATED TO WALK
IN THE SUPER-REALM WITH GOD

I want you to notice that when the devil was condemned by God to the level of carnality, mankind was sentenced to that realm, too. Until then, man had been walking in the super-realm with God. Let me explain.

When God first made man out of the dust of the ground, He added His super ability. So in the beginning, man never was just a carnal man; he was a super man. But then Adam messed up by giving himself over to the Serpent and his deception.

When that happened, Satan lost his super ability and became carnal. When man failed God, he lost the part that had made him super, and he became carnal. Then everybody was on the same level.

Satan is called **the god of this world** (2 Corinthians 4:4).

What world?

The carnal world, the fleshly world. Psalm 24:1 says, **The earth is the Lord's, and the fulness thereof**. But Satan is the god of this world's system.

JESUS CAME DOWN ON SATAN'S LEVEL

The Bible tells us that the Word became flesh and dwelt among men (John 1:14). The Word, Jesus, came down on the level where everybody else was. That is the only way Satan could have tempted Him; he had no authority to tempt Jesus on that higher level.

So, Jesus came down on Satan's level, and He was made subject to everything you and I are subject to in this world. Think about every sin you have ever committed in your life and realize that Jesus was subject to those same temptations.

If Jesus had come to earth and had totally annihilated the works of the devil, He would have removed that carnality forever. That means we would not be seeing it anymore. But have you seen any carnality lately? You probably saw some today.

So, it didn't mean that sins were totally wiped away. But you were given a way to be set free from sin, a way to come out of the flesh. Then you could be free from the works of the devil — free from carnality.

This is the purpose of Jesus: to make a way so that you, the believer, don't have to be subject to what Satan is subject to in this carnal realm.

Jesus came to loose you from the works of the devil, like somebody in chains can be set free. You have been walking around bound by the flesh, bound by carnality. But Jesus said, "I came to give you the keys of the Kingdom. It is the Father's pleasure to give you the Kingdom." (Matthew 16:19; Luke 12:32.)

WHEN JESUS FACED THE TEMPTER

Now look at Matthew 4:1:

Then was Jesus led up of the Spirit into the wilderness to be tempted of the devil.

Who is doing the tempting here? The devil.

And when he had fasted forty days and forty nights, he was afterward an hungred (v. 2).

For Jesus to be fasting forty days and forty nights was not a carnal thing. If you were going into the wilderness, you would take some food. Man has to eat.

Satan said to Jesus, "Wait a minute. You are on my realm. When You don't eat on my realm, You get hungry."

But Jesus was saying, "I can't do what you do in your realm. By doing that, I would become subject to your realm."

Now look at Matthew 4:3:

And when the tempter came to him, he said, If thou be the Son of God, command that these stones be made bread.

Where does doubt work? In the carnal realm.

The tempter said to Him, *If* **thou be the Son of God....** The Serpent came to Eve with the same doubt, saying, **Yea, hath God said...?** (Genesis 3:1).

Satan knew Who Jesus was. But I want you to notice what Jesus was doing here. He was saying: "I came on the level of man to show man how to get out. For Me to do something that man can't do would be illegal. Even though I am God, while I am on man's level, I can't operate as God; I have to operate as a man."

We see Jesus' response to the devil in Matthew 4:4:

But he answered and said, It is written....

The devil wanted Jesus to be like a magician and do some magic tricks. But Jesus was trying to show us something here. Notice what He does in the midst of this carnal, fleshly temptation: He immediately goes to God's Word. Here's the greatest key Jesus gives us:

...It is written, Man shall not live by bread alone, but by every word that proceedeth out of the mouth of God (v. 4).

Jesus is showing us the way out of temptation: to live by the Word of God. He says, **Man shall not live by bread alone, but by every word that proceedeth out of the mouth of God.**

Now look at Matthew 4, verses 5 and 6:

Then the devil taketh him up into the holy city, and setteth him on a pinnacle of the temple,

And saith unto him, If thou be the Son of God, cast thyself down: for it is written....

The devil was saying, "All right, if You can go to that written Word, then I can go there, too."

In verse 6 Satan continues:

...for it is written, He shall give his angels charge concerning thee: and in their hands they shall bear thee up, lest at any time thou dash thy foot against a stone.

These words can be found in Psalm 91:11. So this proves the devil knows the Bible.

Matthew 4:7 shows Jesus responding to the devil with more of God's Word:

Jesus said unto him, It is written again, Thou shalt not tempt the Lord thy God.

What was Jesus saying?

"Devil, I am operating on a level that has authority over the level you operate on. Although you use the Word, it won't work on your level; it will only work on My level."

God's Word won't work when we are in the flesh. As Galatians 6:8 says, **He that soweth to his flesh shall of the flesh reap corruption; but he that soweth to the Spirit shall of the Spirit reap life everlasting.** You can't sow spiritual things in fleshly soil and expect to get results. So, even though the devil said, "It is written," he was saying it from a different level than Jesus.

Now look at Matthew 4:8:

Again, the devil taketh him up into an exceeding high mountain, and sheweth him all the kingdoms of the world, and the glory of them.

I want you to realize this would not have been called a temptation had Jesus not been lured to yield to it. You see, I could never be tempted to get pregnant; as a male, it would be physically impossible.

Obviously, these were serious temptations against Jesus. But this third one was the chiefest. The devil took Him up on top of that mountain and showed Him the very kingdoms he had stolen from God, which was exactly why Jesus had come. The devil was saying, "Come here. I know what You want. Look and see."

So, the devil is showing Jesus all the kingdoms of the world and the glory of them, then he goes on in verse 9:

And saith unto him, All these things will I give thee [he should have said, "Give back to thee"], *if thou wilt fall down and worship me.*

Jesus couldn't fall *down* unless He was up somewhere. Satan was saying to Him, "Come on down where I am; fall down here on my level and worship me."

Now realize the significance of this. The only reason this temptation went on as long as it did is so that we would be able to teach about it today. I want you to see this. Look at Matthew 4:10,11:

Then saith Jesus unto him, Get thee hence, Satan: for it is written, Thou shalt worship the Lord thy God, and him only shalt thou serve.

Then the devil leaveth him, and, behold, angels came and ministered unto him.

Notice the devil left Him right then.

YOUR AUTHORITY IN JESUS' NAME

When you operate in authority from the Spirit — when you speak to the devil and his greatest temptation — everything in the carnal realm is made subject to your authority because of where it comes from and Who it represents. When you stand in the authority of Jesus' name as an ambassador of the Anointed One and His anointing, you can command the devil to leave — and he must go!

What am I saying? You don't have to put up with the devil for even a split second. Why? Because of where you live — in Jesus. If you are tired of the devil, tell him to leave. If you are fed up with him being in your finances, tell him to go. If he is in your household, command him to depart.

But you can't be continuing to live in the carnal realm when you are trying to stand against the devil. If you do that, he will only say, "I have a right to be here."

Let's take it a little further now. I want you to see how you aren't missing it when you spend all this time in the Word by meditating on it, by speaking it, by living it and practicing it.

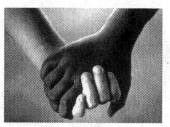

CHAPTER 13

JESUS AND THE HIGHER LIFE

We just finished looking at Jesus as a Man Who was anointed of God. We saw how He handled temptations in His life. Let's look now at First Corinthians 10:12,13:

Wherefore let him that thinketh he standeth take heed lest he fall.

There hath no temptation taken you....

Remember who the tempter is: Satan. I believe we can safely assume, then, that the temptation referred to here is coming from the devil.

THESE TEMPTATIONS ARE COMMON TO MAN

Continuing in First Corinthians 10, verse 13, it says:

There hath no temptation taken you but such as is common to man....

What is the apostle Paul saying here? That there is no test or trial that can come to you, the believer, except what is common to man. That the tempter (Satan) can't use anything super to try to get at you. Whatever he uses against you has to be common to man. In other words, it has to take place within this physical realm.

So just remember, you aren't the only person to have experienced the kind of temptations and snares from the devil that you have.

Somebody somewhere on this earth has been through those same tests and trials.

Temptation has to come on the level of the flesh, of carnality, because that is the area to which the tempter has been confined. As we saw in the book of Genesis, the Serpent was condemned by God to crawl on his belly in the dust. That is when Satan's power was restricted by God to operate only on the level of carnality, of the flesh.

YOUR WEAPONS OF WARFARE AS A BELIEVER

Now let me show you what God has made available to you as a believer in Jesus. Look at Second Corinthians 10:3:

For though we walk in the flesh, we do not war after the flesh.

Fleshly things operate in the realm of the flesh, but that is not where we war. So, don't fight the devil on his own battleground. Why? Verse 4 tells us:

For the weapons of our warfare are not carnal, but mighty through God to the pulling down of strong holds.

Here the apostle Paul is describing a weapon that is strong enough to pull down strongholds. These "strongholds" reside in the minds of men. That's where Satan is given the opportunity to function. One of the most powerful weapons the devil uses against man is suggestion.

God is speaking to you, the believer, and is saying: "I have provided you with weaponry that can pull down Satan's strongholds." He says you have been given weapons that are not carnal.

So remember, Satan's weapons are carnal; his resources are fleshly and devilish. The believer's weapons are mighty through God to the pulling down of strongholds. God has not intended for His children to war with carnal, fleshly weapons. If you try to fight this warfare in the carnal realm, you will only be defeated by the god of this world.

Continuing in Second Corinthians 10, verses 5 and 6, we read:

Casting down imaginations, and every high thing that exalteth itself against the knowledge of God, and bringing into captivity every thought to the obedience of Christ;

And having in a readiness to revenge all disobedience, when your obedience is fulfilled.

In other words, this is saying: "You, the believer, are to be bringing everything down to the obedience of the Anointed One and His anointing."

LIVING ABOVE THIS EARTHLY REALM

Let's look again at Romans, chapter 8, verses 1 and 2:

There is therefore now no condemnation to them which are in Christ Jesus [the Anointed One and His anointing], who walk not after the flesh, but after the Spirit.

For the law of the Spirit of life in Christ Jesus [or in the Word] hath made me free from the law of sin and death [or from carnality].

Do you know what Jesus did? He stripped Satan of his authority and his power — all of it!

In Luke 10:19 Jesus said to His followers:

Behold, I give unto you power to tread on serpents and scorpions, and over all the power of the enemy: and nothing shall by any means hurt you.

Nothing shall hurt you — as long as you do not remain in that realm of carnality. You have to step out of the fleshly realm and over into the spiritual realm. It is the Word versus the flesh.

So, how do you get out of the flesh?

By following God's Word.

The law of the Spirit of life in Christ Jesus has made you free from the law of sin and death. That means God has now introduced a new set of laws for you to operate in. Instead of living in the flesh, you can now rise above the flesh by operating in God's Word. You will no longer be held subject to your flesh; your flesh will be made subject to the Word of the living God.

What does all of this mean?

It means when you were born into this carnal world, you were condemned to the level of carnality; but Jesus came to lift you out of that carnality. When you accepted Him as the sacrificial Lamb Who died on the cross for your sins, that means the Word elevated you out of this realm where Satan operates and put you above the law of sin and death.

It means you are no longer subject to the law of sin and death. Instead, you now have the ability, through the law of life in Christ Jesus, to change the laws of the flesh and to make those laws subject to the law of the Spirit.

"THE DEVIL CAN'T TOUCH YOU NOW!"

The law of the Spirit has made you free from the law of the flesh. Why? So that you can have dominion and absolute mastery over your flesh. You can tread on your flesh, and the devil can't touch you now! That is scriptural. First John 5:18 says:

We know that whosoever is born of God sinneth not; but he that is begotten of God keepeth himself, and that wicked one toucheth him not.

So anytime the devil threatens you, just look at him and say, "You can't touch me!"

Again, First Corinthians 10:13 says:

There hath no temptation taken you but such as is common to man: but God is faithful, who will not suffer [or allow] *you to be tempted* [or tested] *above that ye are able; but will with the temptation also make a way to escape, that ye may be able to bear it.*

Do you know what that "way to escape" is? Jesus said, **I am the way** (John 14:6). The "way to escape" is the Word of the living God.

As First Corinthians 10:13 says, Satan is condemned to use only what is common to man. But God has turned it around for you and me, as believers in Jesus. He lets us use what is uncommon to man. Our weapons are not carnal; they are mighty through God!

Any person here on earth can begin to operate on the level of life in Christ Jesus and be made free from Satan and the ways of this carnal world.

JESUS LIVED BY GOD'S LAW

When I was reading and studying this, I thought about Jesus walking on the water. He came to earth and lived on the same level as man, but He didn't operate by the laws of this natural world. He operated strictly by the laws of God's Word.

You will never see Jesus operating or making Himself subject to the laws that govern this natural world.

There was a time when He was on a boat that got caught in a storm out at sea. He was sleeping through the storm, so the disciples out of fear woke Him. But He refused to give in to the laws of this natural world. Instead, He stood and rebuked that wind; then He said to the sea, **Peace, be still** (Mark 4:39). The forces of this natural world had to submit to His command. Verse 39 says, **And the wind ceased, and there was a great calm.**

There was another time when over 5,000 people had followed Him out into a desert place and He was moved with compassion to minister to their needs. When the time to eat had passed, He believed God to feed that multitude. With only five loaves and two fishes in their supply, He prayed for God to multiply the food they had. After all those people had been fed, there were twelve baskets full of leftovers. (Mark 6:35-44.)

Jesus *never* made Himself subject to the laws governing this natural world. What do we see Him doing? Operating strictly by the law of the Word.

Why did He choose to operate by the law of the Word? In order to change the laws of this natural world.

The laws of the natural are always subject to the laws of the Spirit. Why? Because the natural comes from the Spirit.

Jesus was saying: "I am now a part of the natural, but I will operate only by the law of the Spirit, which made this natural world. The law of the Spirit, the Word, makes Me free from the law of the natural."

YOU CAN LIVE ABOVE THIS NATURAL WORLD

There are circumstances that have occurred in your life because you have subjected yourself to the laws of this natural world. As long as you live and feel in the natural realm, you will think there is nothing you can do about it.

But you are wrong.

Here is where you have to take off the brakes in your mind. The laws of this natural world are subject to the law of God's Word.

You, in this natural world, must begin to operate by the law of God's Word. Then the law of the Word will cause the laws of this natural world to be made subject to you, instead of you being subject to them.

Maybe the laws of this world are declaring that you have cancer and are going to die as a result of it. Don't subject yourself to operating the way the world operates. Come up higher and operate by the spiritual laws that govern this natural world.

If change is needed, that change can come — but not by dealing with the laws of the natural world; by dealing with the laws of the Spirit. The laws of God's Word will change the laws of this world. Instead of you being subject to the laws of this world, you can now be in authority over those natural laws.

EXAMPLE OF AUTHORITY

What happened to the law of gravity when Jesus stepped out of the boat and put His foot on that water? It had to bow down to the law of the Word. Gravity ceased to exist, because Jesus was operating in a higher level of existence. Gravity had to say, "I subject myself to the law of the Word."

I will show you how it operated. In Matthew 14 Peter saw Jesus walking on the water and he said, "Let me do it." Then Jesus (the Word) said to Peter, "Come." When Jesus spoke that word, it was law, and Peter could begin to walk on the water. Gravity became subject to the law that Peter had obeyed.

When you obey the law of the Spirit — the law of the Word — then the laws of this natural world will have to act unusual. They can't do what they normally do, because you are no longer obeying them. You now are rebelling against those natural laws in order to comply with the law of the Word.

Gravity could not work because Peter did not make himself subject to its law; he made himself subject to the law of Jesus. When Jesus said, "Come," Peter became subject to that word.

THEN PETER'S ATTENTION GOT CHANGED

Satan said, "Oh dear, that boy is walking above my realm, and I am losing control. So, let's throw some wind in there and make those waves move."

Now here is the key:

Peter's attention had been on the law of God, and he wasn't paying any attention to the laws of the natural.

But then what happened?

The laws of the natural changed, and that got his attention. When he realized what was going on around him, he immediately became subject to the laws that govern this natural world.

THE HIGHER LAW IS SPEAKING

How do we get out of this natural realm? We have to stop giving our attention to the natural laws as Peter did. We have to start paying more attention to the law of life in Christ Jesus. That law of life is what will set us free from the laws of sin and death.

Gravity is something that works all the time, but it had to bow down to the law of the Word spoken by Jesus. Gravity said, "Even though I am a law in this natural world, there is another law higher than me. When that higher law speaks, I have to listen."

God has already spoken, and Jesus only says what God has said. That is why, as we read in Romans 8:5, the Word says:

For they that are after the flesh do mind the things of the flesh; but they that are after the Spirit the things of the Spirit.

To mind means to obey, so obedience is the key. This verse is saying: "They that are after the flesh obey the things of the flesh, and they that are after the Spirit obey the things of the Spirit."

Think about it: when Peter was walking on the water, what was he minding?

If you are sitting around saying, "I'm broke; I don't have any money," then you are making yourself subject to laws that operate in carnality. What you have to do is to say: "Lord, You said You would give seed to the sower and bread to the hungry. I am a sower, and I know I have needs to be met, so I'm going to give according to Your Word." That's how you receive from God.

There is spiritual law that goes against every law in this natural world, which says you can't have it. That natural law has to become subject to the spiritual law that says you can have it.

If you will mind God's Word more than you mind what is in this natural realm, you will begin to receive things from the spiritual world and will start changing things in this natural world.

If you are in trouble right now or are being tempted by the devil, here is my answer to you: get off the devil's battleground. Come on up where you belong. You don't have to stay in the devil's arena. If you don't want to keep getting beat up, then get out of the ring.

WALK AND LIVE IN THE SPIRIT

Now you have to realize this may take some time. You have been living in this natural realm all of your life. You have to change your mind and start thinking the way God thinks. (Philippians 2:5.) What God says will work just as quickly and surely as what you have seen going on in this world.

But you can't do that just by going to church once a week or by studying your Bible occasionally. You have to be consistent.

Galatians 5:16 says:

This I say then, Walk in the Spirit, and ye shall not fulfil the lust [or appetite] *of the flesh.*

This verse in *The Amplified Bible* says:

But I say, walk and live [habitually] in the [Holy] Spirit....

In other words, don't just do this every now and then; make living in the Spirit a habit.

But I say, walk and live [habitually] in the [Holy] Spirit [responsive to and controlled and guided by the Spirit]; then you will certainly not gratify the cravings and desires of the flesh (of human nature without God).

For the desires of the flesh are opposed to the [Holy] Spirit, and the [desires of the] Spirit are opposed to the flesh (godless human nature); for these are antagonistic to each other [continually withstanding and in conflict with each other], so that you are not free but are prevented from doing what you desire to do.

But if you are guided (led) by the [Holy] Spirit, you are not subject to the Law.

Galatians 5:16-18 AMP

In other words, verse 18 is saying, "You are not subject to this natural world."

According to Psalm 91:1, you should be living in the secret place of the Most High and abiding under the shadow of the Almighty. When you are in that secret place, you will be protected. You are in the place where the devil can do nothing to you. That's what has made us free.

Do you know what destroys a lot of believers? They are continuing to abide in the carnal world, instead of in that new place God has for them.

What did Jesus say about abiding?

If ye abide in me, and my words abide in you, ye shall ask what ye will, and it shall be done unto you.

John 15:7

LIVING ABOVE CARNALITY

When you are no longer living in the realm of the carnal, there is nothing to stop this process of growing in the Spirit. You are no longer living in the atmosphere where the devil has any power over you. You are living above it. As long as you stay above it, no hindrance can stop you.

If your prayer life is being hindered, do you know why? It is because you are still living in the wrong realm — that carnal, fleshly realm. Come out of it. Come on up into this higher life in Jesus and be spiritual.

When you operate in this spiritual realm, your prayers won't be hindered. Scripture says, God **hath raised us up together, and made us sit together in heavenly places in Christ Jesus** (Ephesians 2:6). Just ask yourself, *Am I operating in His realm?*

Maybe you have been sitting in the wrong place trying to receive all the right things. God just wants to bring you on up, so that you are living above carnality. Then you can sit with Him in heavenly places and learn the laws of God that govern the natural realm here on earth.

How do you do it? By obeying the Word of God in *every* area of your life. God's Word will keep you out of carnality if you are willing to receive it into your life and act on it.

THE NEXT SUBJECT TO BE COVERED

I will be dealing next with a subject which I believe is vital to our walk with God: the power of agreement. The Spirit of God has revealed to me how this aspect of our spiritual walk is under attack, like never before, from the devil and his forces.

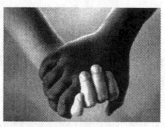

CHAPTER 14

AGREEMENT VS. DIVISION

Satan is out to disrupt the power of agreement in the lives of every born-again child of God. He is trying to demolish agreement in *every* area of our lives — in marriage, in family relationships, in friendships, in business associations, in race relations.

We can be saved, baptized, filled with the Holy Spirit and full of God's Word, yet still allow ourselves to be subject to the techniques and tricks of the devil.

As believers, we may agree on some things, but we let problems, like strife, envy, arguments and fussing, come along and block the path that would have brought God's blessings into our lives. We have allowed that power of agreement to be broken. The power of agreement is haunted by the spirit that causes division.

Amos 3:3 says:

Can two walk together, except they be agreed?

TO AGREE IS TO HARMONIZE

Let's define the word *agree*. To agree means to be in accord, to have harmony, to be of one mind. Simply put, to be in accord means to live in concord, without contention or quarrels. To come together in agreement would be like making a symphony. In a symphony, all available instruments are in harmony.

Now when we are dealing with mankind, there are certain instruments available to us. Man has a spirit; he has a soul, made up of his intellect, or his thinking capacity; and he has a body. For each of us to walk in harmony within ourselves, we have to get our spirit, our soul and our body to agree on what we are trying to do.

Let's say a man goes to church or to a Bible study and hears the Word of God preached in truth. He receives that Word down in his spirit; but then when he goes home, he allows a trick of the devil to change his mind.

What has Satan done? He has successfully disrupted that harmony. So, the devil knows he can defeat God if he can just keep disrupting the harmony among God's people.

Realize this: the devil sees the believer in Jesus as his target against God's move in the earth, so he will immediately start to work against you.

God recognizes that when a man's spirit comes in line with his soul and with his body, that man will be able to walk in the victory God intends for him. But he will never walk in victory when he is out of harmony with himself.

Maybe he received the truth in his spirit when he heard God's Word preached, but then his mind was changed by something he saw or heard on his way home. Maybe he received the truth in his spirit and was willing to accept it in his mind, but his flesh was just too weak to stand strong and to believe God.

Man's triune being — spirit, soul and body — must come together and harmonize as one in order for him to walk in victory with God.

AGREE WITH GOD'S WORD

We must, first of all, come into agreement with God's Word. We have to agree with His Word in our spirit, because spiritual things go with spiritual things. Next, we have to cause our mind to line up with our spirit. Then we must motivate our body to follow suit. We will be unable to agree with other believers until we have established what we are agreeing on.

Husbands and wives who are not living by the Word of God will have a hard time establishing agreement. Why? Because they have no foundation on which to agree in the first place. If they are always living their lives based on their own opinions, then they will seldom agree because they were brought up in different circumstances and situations.

Unless we all, as believers, declare that we are going to live by God's Word, we will have nothing to agree on. The world's system is designed to break the power of agreement.

So, we have to reach the point where we understand that the Word of God becomes the foundation for our agreement. We must refuse to agree with circumstances, or with what was said by another person, or with what we heard reported on the six o'clock news. We have to agree only with God's Word.

With this in mind, I want us to begin looking in chapter 18 of Matthew's gospel and see what Jesus is saying in this chapter. Notice all the different subjects He brings up, and the division and strife that are involved in each situation.

Jesus opens by talking about strife and then discusses humility as the solution to strife. From there, He moves to a description of the power of agreement that has been made available to us as believers. (We have to be determined not to let the devil break that agreement.) Then Jesus talks about the importance of forgiveness.

We will be looking at some of these verses from *The Amplified Bible*, which I believe will make them easier to understand.

STRIFE — CONTENTION — DIVISION

At that time the disciples came up and asked Jesus, Who then is [really] the greatest in the kingdom of heaven?

Matthew 18:1 AMP

I want you to notice how this chapter starts off with the disciples asking Jesus a question that is designed to engender strife. And what does the Bible say about strife? James 3:16 says, **For where envying and strife is, there is confusion and every evil work.** Whenever there is strife, there will be division.

If division is there, can agreement be there?

No.

If strife or contentions are there, can agreement be there?

No.

So, it is amazing that this chapter starts off with the subject of strife when the disciples ask Jesus, "Who is the greatest among us?"

Can you imagine the strife and contentions this must have caused among them, the arguments they must have had?

Peter could have said, "I know I'm the greatest — I walked on water."

But Matthew could have responded to him, "You may have started out that way, but you failed."

Ask yourself: Why did Jesus send the disciples out two by two, as mentioned in Mark 6:7; why didn't He just anoint them and send them out individually? After all, they could have covered much more ground that way.

He sent them out two by two so they would have the power of agreement. Do you see where we are going? The power of God is available when two or more people begin to agree with one another.

(Matthew 18:19.) It is God's best that we learn the importance of agreeing with one another. The "Lone Ranger spirit" that has been at work within the Church must end.

We have to be careful when we talk about who is the greatest, because competitive jealousy can come in very quickly.

That's what strife is. We feel like we have the right to be fussy if we want to be, the right to be touchy if we want to be, the right to just feel bad if we want to.

Then in the middle of this strife-filled situation, Jesus introduces a subject which happens to be the solution to that problem.

JESUS ILLUSTRATES WITH A LITTLE CHILD

And Jesus called a little child unto him, and set him in the midst of them.

Matthew 18:2

Jesus calls a little child to Himself and uses that child as an illustration. This was probably humiliating to the disciples. They were ready to be crowned the greatest by Jesus, and then He calls a little child to be their example.

They may have looked at that child and said: "This little kid hasn't been working with us. We don't know him. He hasn't travelled with us. He can't preach like us. He can't pray like us. Who does he think he is? The little squirt!"

Watch how Jesus uses this child as a way to slap down their pride and to deal with their egos, their strife, their envy and their jealousy. This is a fact that you don't want to miss.

Truly I say to you, unless you repent (change, turn about) and become like little children... (v. 3 AMP).

Jesus didn't say they were to actually become a little child, but that they were to **become *like* little children**. Notice how that is described in this verse. He says:

Truly I say to you, unless you repent (change, turn about)
and become like little children [trusting, lowly, loving,
forgiving], you can never enter the kingdom of heaven [at all]
(v. 3 AMP).

THE KEY IS HUMILITY

Then He says:

Whoever will humble himself therefore and become like this
little child [trusting, lowly, loving, forgiving] is greatest in the
kingdom of heaven (v. 4 AMP).

The key to becoming as a little child is humility.

So, what is humility? What does it mean to humble yourself and take on Bible humility? If we don't know how to humble ourselves, we will never know how to become like that little child.

Being humble means to submit to, to comply with and to obey the orders of the one who has authority over you.

When I began to do a study on the Greek word translated "agree," I found synonyms such as submit, obey and comply. So, that's what humility is: agreeing with God.

BUT THERE IS FALSE HUMILITY

Let me show you the difference between false humility and true humility.

With false humility we say, "We deserve hell." Is that an agreement with God? No. God says we deserve heaven.

With false humility we say, "Oh, we are so unrighteous. There is none righteous; no, not one." Is that agreement with God? No. God says we are made the righteousness of God.

So, what is false humility?

That which does not agree with God.

Now the world has confused true humility with pride and arrogance. Let me show you what true humility is.

Suppose you say, "I am anointed."

Does that sound arrogant to your flesh? Yes.

But does it agree with God? Yes.

Then what is true humility, or Bible humility? The truly humble person is one who agrees with God. This person says: "I am the head and not the tail. I am above, and I never again will be beneath. I have all my needs met according to His riches in glory by Christ Jesus."

Now this doesn't sound good to the fleshly ear. The fleshly ear says you need to sound humble and say, "Oh, Lord, I have nothing but burdens." But that is not the truth, and it is not setting yourself in agreement with God.

When we break our agreement with God, what have we entered into? False humility. We have entered into pride.

AN OLD TESTAMENT EXAMPLE

There is a story in the book of Daniel, where King Nebuchadnezzar refused to agree with God. But God dealt with him.

> *The king spake, and said, Is not this great Babylon, that I have built for the house of the kingdom by the might of my power, and for the honour of my majesty?*

> Daniel 4:30

What was Nebuchadnezzar saying? "I built this house by my own power and my own might, and for my own honor."

While the word was in the king's mouth, there fell a voice from heaven, saying, O king Nebuchadnezzar, to thee it is spoken; The kingdom is departed from thee.

Daniel 4:31

God was saying, "You are not agreeing with Me, so the kingdom has departed from you."

And they shall drive thee from men, and thy dwelling shall be with the beasts of the field: they shall make thee to eat grass as oxen, and seven times shall pass over thee, until thou know that the most High ruleth in the kingdom of men, and giveth it to whomsoever he will.

Daniel 4:32

Nebuchadnezzar obviously didn't agree with God on this, because he thought he was king and he was the ruler there. But God was in control.

The same hour was the thing fulfilled upon Nebuchadnezzar: and he was driven from men, and did eat grass as oxen, and his body was wet with the dew of heaven, till his hairs were grown like eagles' feathers, and his nails like birds' claws.

Daniel 4:33

Now look at what happened next:

And at the end of the days I Nebuchadnezzar lifted up mine eyes unto heaven, and mine understanding returned unto me, and I blessed the most High, and I praised and honoured him that liveth for ever, whose dominion is an everlasting dominion, and his kingdom is from generation to generation:

And all the inhabitants of the earth are reputed as nothing: and he doeth according to his will in the army of heaven, and among the inhabitants of the earth: and none can stay his hand, or say unto him, What doest thou?

At the same time my reason returned unto me; and for the glory of my kingdom, mine honour and brightness returned unto me; and my counsellors and my lords sought unto me; and I was established in my kingdom, and excellent majesty was added unto me.

Now I Nebuchadnezzar praise and extol and honour the King of heaven, all whose works are truth, and his ways judgment: and those that walk in pride he is able to abase.

Daniel 4:34-37

I would end verse 37 like this: "And those who walk in disagreement, God is able to bring down."

BE CAREFUL WHO YOU AGREE WITH

Let's look again in Matthew, chapter 18. Verses 4 and 5 AMP say:

Whoever will humble himself therefore and become like this little child [trusting, lowly, loving, forgiving] is greatest in the kingdom of heaven.

And whoever receives and accepts and welcomes one little child like this for My sake and in My name receives and accepts and welcomes Me.

Did you catch what Jesus is saying here?

He says, "When you agree with those who agree with Me, then you are agreeing with Me."

That's why you have to be careful who you agree with. Don't pray with somebody who hasn't even made up his mind whether or not he agrees with the Word of God.

Suppose you are trying to get a new car, and that other person isn't even sure if God can do it. If he isn't in agreement with the Word, what makes you think his agreement with you is going to work?

So, Jesus is saying, "Agree with those who agree with Me, and you will be agreeing with Me."

ENTICEMENT WILL COME

Matthew 18:6 AMP says:

But whoever causes one of these little ones who believe in and acknowledge and cleave to Me to stumble and sin [that is, who entices him or hinders him in right conduct or thought]....

Notice that this person is in agreement with God. He is living according to God's Word and doing what God tells him to do. But then another person comes along and entices him.

Maybe that person says something like, "There's nothing wrong with smoking a reefer; God doesn't mind if you get high a little bit," or "There's nothing wrong with having sex before marriage; the two of you are getting married anyway, so you might as well go ahead and try it out."

Jesus is saying there will be judgment on those who entice and seduce and cause others to fall away. One person has made up his mind to agree with God, then someone else comes along and disrupts that agreement by enticing that individual and breaking the agreement he had with God.

Look at the judgment Jesus talks about in Matthew 18:6 AMP:

...it would be better (more expedient and profitable or advantageous) for him to have a great millstone fastened around his neck and to be sunk in the depth of the sea.

I want you to notice what Jesus says in the next verse. He is warning the world.

Woe to the world for such temptations to sin and influences to do wrong! It is necessary that temptations come, but woe to the person on whose account or by whom the temptation comes!

Matthew 18:7 AMP

He is saying, "Woe to you for such solicitations to sin!"

STAND AGAINST SIN

Then in verse 8 AMP Jesus says:

And if your hand or your foot causes you to stumble and sin, cut it off and throw it away from you....

He is saying, "It isn't worth letting what you want to do break the agreement you have with Me." He goes on in this verse:

...it is better (more profitable and wholesome) for you to enter life maimed or lame than to have two hands or two feet and be thrown into everlasting fire (v. 8 AMP).

Which is better — to enter into heaven without ever having known the enjoyment of sin, or to enjoy sin immensely now in this life and be thrown into hell's fire?

Do you actually think you can continue to sin day after day, week after week, year after year, and not have God's judgment to come upon you? If so, you would be wrong.

As a minister of God's Word, I wouldn't want to be living in sin, and then enter the pulpit to preach the Word. I could fall dead right there.

How could you think it would be more profitable to continue sinning?

Somebody says, "But it feels good."

Of course it feels good; if it didn't, it wouldn't be enticing. It wouldn't be a temptation if it didn't have some feeling of pleasure with it.

SATAN'S GOAL:
TO BREAK THE POWER OF AGREEMENT

I want you to realize this: everything the devil does is designed to break your power of agreement.

What is that temptation for? To get you out of agreement with God.

The devil is saying: "You don't have to agree with God. Come over here and agree with me. You don't have to be so holy. Come try this out. You can repent later."

Now it's true that God is faithful and just to forgive you of your sins and to cleanse you of all unrighteousness. That's what the Bible says in First John 1:9. But I want to remind you that when you choose to step into sin you have broken the power of agreement with God. That agreement will be disrupted, hindered and then stopped.

Yes, God will forgive you, but you will be riding on a roller coaster, going up and down, around and around, and never really getting anywhere in your life. If you agree with God, but then break that agreement, you will be wondering why you never get anywhere.

Then condemnation gets in the picture. When you break the agreement, you start condemning yourself. God says, "I have forgiven you," but you can't find a way to agree with Him and forgive yourself. So what can He do? Nothing.

We must be holy as He is holy. Jesus is coming back for a Church without spot or wrinkle. (Ephesians 5:27.)

THE DEVIL MANEUVERS WITH SIN

Let's look now in Matthew 18:9 AMP:

And if your eye causes you to stumble and sin, pluck it out and throw it away from you....

Most sin can be traced back to the eye, the ear and the hand. So what is Jesus saying here? We have to cut off the initial seed — what affects the eye, what affects the ear, what affects the hand.

Do you know what He is saying? He is talking about separation. Watching pornography on TV all night long will cause you to lust all day the next day at work. Let's use some mathematics here. Lust minus pornography equals deliverance. You have to cut off that sin by making a quality decision. Stop it by saying, "That's enough!" It would be like putting a bit in your mouth.

But when you say that, the devil will tempt you some more, saying, "Aw, come on — just one more time. Didn't you enjoy that? Didn't it feel good? Come on."

You just have to be strong and refuse to give in to the devil's maneuvers.

Jesus continues in Matthew 18:9 AMP:

...it is better (more profitable and wholesome) for you to enter life with only one eye than to have two eyes and be thrown into the hell (Gehenna) of fire.

Now look at verses 10-14 AMP:

Beware that you do not despise or feel scornful toward or think little of one of these little ones, for I tell you that in heaven their angels always are in the presence of and look upon the face of My Father Who is in heaven.

For the Son of man came to save [from the penalty of eternal death] that which was lost.

What do you think? If a man has a hundred sheep, and one of them has gone astray and gets lost, will he not leave the ninety-nine on the mountain and go in search of the one that is lost?

And if it should be that he finds it, truly I say to you, he rejoices more over it than over the ninety-nine that did not get lost.

Just so it is not the will of My Father Who is in heaven that one of these little ones should be lost and perish.

The one who was lost had nobody to agree with. The ninety-nine were all right because they had total agreement. This is an example of the mercy of God.

THE STEPS TO WIN BACK AGREEMENT

In Matthew 18:15 AMP we see what to do when something is messing up the agreement between two believers. Jesus tells us what He wants us to do for the sake of the power of agreement:

If your brother wrongs you, go and show him his fault, between you and him privately....

If this brother does or says something to make you mad or to hurt you, no matter how big or small it may be, you aren't to go to somebody else and complain about it; you are to go to that brother by yourself and talk to him about it.

If you were to go gossiping about it to somebody else, you would be starting confusion and allowing strife to come in; then every evil work could come along behind it.

And don't go complaining about it to your pastor. It would be out of order for you to go to your pastor before you go to that person.

You know, we would have a lot more peace if the person who was wronged would just take it upon himself to go and confront his brother for peace rather than for argument. A lot of people think that confrontation is argument, but confrontation is for peace. I would rather have someone come directly to me and tell me my fault than for me to hear it from a third party.

Jesus describes the value of your step in Matthew 18:15 AMP:

...If he listens to you, you have won back your brother.

This means you have won back your brother — *and* your power of agreement.

WHEN DEALING WITH A REBELLIOUS PERSON

Then Jesus applies the power of agreement to the rebellious person who doesn't want to listen.

But if he does not listen, take along with you one or two others, so that every word may be confirmed and upheld by the testimony of two or three witnesses.

Matthew 18:16 AMP

At this point, it's important that you find one or two others who will join together in agreement with you. You are agreeing together that, according to the Word of God, what that other person did was absolutely wrong. Then you go to that person, and each of you says to him, "I love you, but you were wrong." There is a better chance that he will listen to you now because of the power of agreement among you.

As a pastor, I am telling you that you had better go through this procedure. It would be wrong for you to come to me before you go first by yourself and then, if necessary, take others with you.

If he pays no attention to them [refusing to listen and obey], tell it to the church....

Matthew 18:17 AMP

Now we are adding more agreement by bringing it before the Church and having the local body to agree. Look at the rest of verse 17 AMP and see what Jesus says:

...and if he refuses to listen even to the church, let him be to you as a pagan and a tax collector.

Do you realize what Jesus has said here? You are to treat that person the way you would a sinner. Why? Because he is in sin.

The power of agreement may very well win back that person. When he sees that his whole spiritual family has withdrawn fellowship from him, all of a sudden it might click inside him that he is wrong. Then he will say, "I was wrong. Please forgive me."

THE IMPORTANCE OF AGREEMENT
BETWEEN CHURCH MEMBERS

Now, church members are supposed to be people who agree, not people who disagree and gossip and try to tear down what their church is striving to accomplish. Every time we allow dissention, strife, envy and jealousy to come within our local church bodies, the power of agreement will be affected. The process won't be stopped as long as there are always believers who will agree. But the results could be really awesome if the power of agreement was allowed to work unhindered.

I just wish all those who do not agree within their church would leave. Why should they hang around?

If I were a member of a church and didn't agree with what was going on, I would either get help so that I could understand, or leave. I wouldn't stay and keep talking about it, trying to figure it out. That would just be causing dissention and contention and strife.

So, don't get yourself out of agreement in your church and wonder why nothing is happening in your own life. Just move on and find a church where you can agree with your fellow brothers and sisters in Christ.

That happened to me one time in a church I was attending. Disagreeing with the pastor, I got into trouble by rebelling in certain ways. I had been acting like an idiot and a fool, and judgment came upon me. At that time in my life, I really didn't know any better, which is probably why the mercy of God was there.

We left and started another church, and it was growing, but something was missing. Then I realized nothing would ever be right in my life or in my ministry because I had sinned against my previous pastor and his church. The Lord said, "Son, I can't do anything I have showed you until you go there and repent before that pastor and his entire congregation."

I went to the pastor's office, grabbed his hands and looked at him with tears in my eyes. Now I didn't just say, "If I did anything wrong, please forgive me." *I accepted the responsibility for my actions.*

I said to him: "I have sinned before you, before God and before this church. I have rebelled and operated in sedition and division, and I have spoken against you. Please forgive me if you can."

Then he broke down in tears and said, "I esteem you higher than I have esteemed any man I have ever known."

There were guests at his church that night and they were having a big meeting, but I got up before all those people and said: "My name is Creflo A. Dollar Jr., and I have sinned. I rebelled against the pastor of this church, and I caused division and sedition in this body. I was wrong, and he was right. So now I ask this church to forgive me."

The anointing of God fell in that place, and everybody on the platform began to weep. Then miracles began to take place in the congregation.

Once I had hooked back up into my place of agreement, God could shower me with the anointing. That is why He talks against rebellion and against sins of the mouth, like gossip and backbiting. All these things will affect the power of agreement.

There are two things the Lord told me about the mouth: it can be an asset or it can be our greatest enemy. Scripture says, **Death and life are in the power of the tongue: and they that love it shall eat the fruit thereof** (Proverbs 18:21). How you exercise your tongue now will determine whether or not you love it.

CHAPTER 15

AGREEMENT — UNITY — FORGIVENESS

Now, let's go further in Matthew, chapter 18. There is something interesting that takes place in verse 18. Jesus says:

Verily I say unto you, Whatsoever ye shall bind on earth shall be bound in heaven: and whatsoever ye shall loose on earth shall be loosed in heaven.

For some reason, we have gotten the idea that once we have bound something here on earth, then it will be bound in heaven. This was my thinking for a long time, and it probably is your thinking too, if you will be honest about it. But that idea goes totally against spiritual order. The truth is, everything that exists in this physical world must first exist in the spirit world.

Let's read this verse from *The Amplified Bible* and look at it carefully:

Truly I tell you, whatever you forbid and declare to be improper and unlawful on earth must be what is already forbidden in heaven, and whatever you permit and declare proper and lawful on earth must be what is already permitted in heaven.

Jesus says if you forbid something on this earth, it must already be forbidden in accordance with God's Word. You can't declare, "I bind this in the earth," if God hasn't already bound it in heaven. You can't say, "I loose this in the earth," if God hasn't already loosed it in heaven.

SO, WHAT IS MEANT BY BINDING AND LOOSING?

Binding and loosing are what we do on earth by agreeing with what God has already done in heaven. What we bind on earth agrees with what God has bound; what we loose on earth agrees with what God has loosed. So, what we see here on earth must already have been established in heaven.

My binding or loosing of things is my agreeing with what has already taken place in heaven, or in heavenly places. Simplified, I agree with what has already taken place in the Word of God. I can't go around binding and loosing things that God hasn't already settled. Do you understand what I am saying? My authority as a believer must be within the boundaries of God's Word.

Sometimes we think we can step out of those boundaries, especially in prayer. But when Scripture says you can ask whatsoever you will, it means you can ask whatsoever you will — when what you ask is within the boundaries of God's will.

So, our asking, our binding, our loosing is to be according to the Word of God.

Now in the area of binding and loosing, think about what God has bound: He has bound the devil; He has bound sickness; He has bound poverty.

In whatever area God has bound, He is saying to the believer: "Now I need for you to agree with what I have already done in heaven by binding it on earth. I have put you there so that you could agree with Me and be My establishing witness on earth. If you will agree with Me, then together we can build and establish some things to fulfill My will."

In whatever area God has loosed, He is saying to the believer: "Now I need for you to agree with Me by loosing on the earth what I have already loosed in heaven. I have already loosed the angels on your behalf, so go ahead and loose them there. All that needs to be activated to fulfill My will in the earth is your agreement to do what I have already established in heaven."

Scripture says agreement requires only two parties. So, if one is on earth and one is in heaven, that's really all we need.

Suppose somebody says, "My prayer partner is not at home; I don't have anybody to agree with me."

Well, God is always at home. Hallelujah!

Isn't it wonderful to know that when you call God, you won't get one of those answering services where someone says, "One moment please," and then puts you on hold; or one of those computerized systems with the voice that says, "Press this number for this, or that number for that." When you go to God and pray in accordance with His Word, He will always be there to answer your call personally.

What if all of the Bible believers in the entire world decided to call God at the same time? I haven't yet figured out how He could do it, but He would answer *all* of our calls!

HOW SATAN TAKES ADVANTAGE OF AGREEMENT

I want you to see the picture of agreement that Jesus is talking about here in Matthew 18:18. But as we had read previously, Jesus is also talking about agreement in verse 16. Let's look at that verse again:

But if he will not hear thee, then take with thee one or two more, that in the mouth of two or three witnesses every word may be established.

Matthew 18:16

How can every word be established? Because they agree. There are two or three witnesses who are operating in agreement.

For some reason, people like to take certain verses from the Bible and then operate outside of the Word. They can't do that and still expect it to come to pass.

God is not in the business of bringing the devil's words to pass; He is in the business of bringing His own Word to pass. Agreement is established when two or three are harmonizing around God's Word.

So, if you and one or two others are trying to agree outside the boundaries of God's Word, then God will not participate; He will not be in your midst.

But guess who will be glad to participate in your agreement? The devil. What God won't do, the devil is just waiting to do; he operates on the perverted side.

Satan didn't create the power of agreement, but he certainly will take advantage of it if you start agreeing and adding harmony to your sickness, to your problems and to your hard times.

TRUE AGREEMENT IN GOD'S WORD

Now let's go on in Matthew 18:

Again I say unto you, That if two of you shall agree on earth as touching any thing that they shall ask (within the boundaries of God's Word), *it shall be done for them of my Father which is in heaven.*

Matthew 18:19

Jesus begins this verse by saying, *Again* I say unto you....
Could it be that this entire chapter has been about what He is going
to tell us again?

> *Again I tell you, if two of you on earth agree (harmonize*
> *together, make a symphony together) about whatever [anything*
> *and everything] they may ask, it will come to pass and be done*
> *for them by My Father in heaven.*
>
> Matthew 18:19 AMP

Now if we put together three of these verses from Matthew 18 —
verses 16, 18 and 19 — we will see something here.

As Jesus says in verse 16, **In the mouth of two or three witnesses
every word may be established.** He is talking here about bringing
correction to a brother. Based on what He says about how to handle
this situation, He is saying, "If two or three of you are agreeing on the
Word, I will be in the midst of it." But if two or three of you are
agreeing to try to destroy a person or to make that person look bad,
God will never be a part of such a mess.

As Jesus says in verse 18: **Whatever you forbid and declare to be
improper and unlawful on earth must be what is already forbidden
in heaven, and whatever you permit and declare proper and lawful
on earth must be what is already permitted in heaven** (AMP).

This is the believers' agreement with heaven. Whatever we are
binding on earth is already bound in heaven. Whatever we can do on
earth is what can be done in heaven. It is our agreement with heaven
that will give us the manifestation here on earth. And how do we
agree with heaven? By agreeing with the Word.

Jesus then begins verse 19 by saying, **Again I say unto you....** He
has not broken the subject matter; He is continuing to talk about the
power of agreement.

He says, **Again I say unto you...**, then He says it in a different way: **That if two of you shall agree on earth as touching any thing that they shall ask....** What are the boundaries of our asking? The Word of God.

Somebody says, "The Word says we can agree and just ask for anything." But we can't just be taking these principles without really knowing how to operate them. I will give you an example.

AGREEING WITH GOD'S WORD

Let's say you are wanting a brother in the Lord to agree with you about getting a new car. But before doing that, are you sure you have received a *rhema* word about it? Let me explain.

It isn't that God would mind you having a new car. But there is something called *rhema*[1], a word from God that is spoken or revealed to your heart by the Spirit of God. Then you would be convinced in your heart that this is what God has said about the situation.

You should not just agree about getting a car without having acknowledged God in all of your ways so that He could direct your path. (Proverbs 3:5,6.) Then you will have that *rhema* word to stand on. The *rhema* word must agree with the written Word, the *logos*[2].

If a *rhema* word comes to you in prayer, it must always agree with the written Word of God. If it does not do that, then it was not a *rhema* word — it was not from God, but from somewhere else.

If God is telling us the importance of agreement, why should He Himself break agreement with His Word? What would it look like if you said God had told you this, but the Word completely contradicted

---

[1]Strong, "Greek Dictionary of the New Testament," p. 63, #4487.
[2]Ibid., p. 45, #3056.

what you said? God knows it won't stand if it does not agree with His Word.

So, before you just run off with an inspiration in your heart, make sure you get agreement from the written Word of God. The recommendation must be out of the mouth of two or three witnesses before it is established.

I know people who quit their jobs because they said they had "heard from God." But they didn't hear from God; they heard from their lazy flesh.

AGREEMENT PUTS GOD IN OUR MIDST

Now let's continue on in Matthew, chapter 18. Jesus says:

> *For wherever two or three are gathered (drawn together as My followers) in (into) My name, there I AM in the midst of them.*

Matthew 18:20 AMP

What is Jesus in the midst of? Is He in the midst of us, or is He in the midst of our agreement?

He is in the midst of our agreement when it agrees with Him. That's what He is there for.

I know He will be in the midst of what I have agreed on, because what I have agreed on is what He has already determined in His Word. That's why He is there. He wouldn't be there if my agreement wasn't in line with Him. Do you understand that?

Don't ever get together with someone and try to believe out of line with God's Word, saying something like: "Well, the two of us are here together, believing that the Lord will send us some reefer tonight. So we're just waiting on the Lord."

When you are praying prayers of doubt and unbelief, which are not in line with God's Word, God will not be there. When you are singing songs that don't line up with God's Word, He is not there. When you are "testi-lying" — in effect, stretching the truth to make your personal story sound more interesting — He is not there. God is never there when His Word — His Truth — is not there.

So if you want God in the midst of you, put His Word in the midst of you by coming into agreement with that Word. Then it is guaranteed that He will be in the midst of your agreement.

Why is it that a man can get up and preach a seemingly boring sermon with only the Bible as his base and then see his church grow to 12,000 people?

Because God is there.

Some ministers have the audacity to depend on their own talents and their "speechabilities" to try to draw people to their churches. After a while, those who are seeking the Truth will wonder, "Where is God?"

That's why I can't afford to preach anything but the Word of God. We need Him because we can't do anything without Him. The only way I know to contact God is through His Word.

UNITY THROUGH FORGIVENESS

Notice again Matthew 18:19,20. In verse 19 Jesus says:

Again I say unto you, That if two of you shall agree on earth....

Then in verse 20 He says:

For where two or three are gathered together in my name, there am I in the midst of them.

This demonstrates the power of unity: where two of us shall agree.

If a white man and a black man can come together with another white man and black man, and they can talk reconciliation, Jesus is saying, "I will be there with those who are there to reconcile."

Somebody says, "How do you know it is talking about reconciliation?"

Look what it says in Matthew 18:21 AMP:

Then Peter came up to Him and said, Lord, how many times may my brother sin against me and I forgive him and let it go? [As many as] up to seven times?

Peter thought he was being magnanimous, or overly generous, when he asked Jesus, "Up to seven times?" He thought the Lord would probably say, "No, just two or three." But that's not what the Lord said. Look at verse 22 from *The Amplified Bible*:

Jesus answered him, I tell you, not up to seven times, but seventy times seven!

I want to show you something: "Seventy times seven" equals 490 times a day. In a week, that would be 3,430 times. Now there are 52 weeks in a year, so if you forgive 3,430 times a week, that totals 178,360 times a year. That would be giving somebody a whole lot of leeway.

Jesus says that is how many times we are to forgive!

THE RESULTS OF UNFORGIVENESS

Now when Jesus moves into the subject of unforgiveness here in chapter 18, He tells the very interesting story about a man who received cancellation of his debt but wouldn't cancel the debt owed to him by another man.

Therefore is the kingdom of heaven likened unto a certain king, which would take account of his servants.

And when he had begun to reckon, one was brought unto him, which owed him ten thousand talents.

But forasmuch as he had not to pay, his lord commanded him to be sold, and his wife, and children, and all that he had, and payment to be made.

The servant therefore fell down, and worshipped him, saying, Lord, have patience with me, and I will pay thee all.

Then the lord of that servant was moved with compassion, and loosed him, and forgave him the debt.

Matthew 18:23-27

This is really good. That servant's debt was cancelled! But now look at the rest of the story:

But the same servant went out, and found one of his fellowservants, which owed him an hundred pence: and he laid hands on him, and took him by the throat, saying, Pay me that thou owest.

And his fellowservant fell down at his feet, and besought him, saying, Have patience with me, and I will pay thee all.

And he would not: but went and cast him into prison, till he should pay the debt.

So when his fellowservants saw what was done, they were very sorry, and came and told unto their lord all that was done.

Then his lord, after that he had called him, said unto him, O thou wicked servant, I forgave thee all that debt, because thou desiredst me:

Shouldest not thou also have had compassion on thy fellowservant, even as I had pity on thee?

And his lord was wroth, and delivered him to the tormentors, till he should pay all that was due unto him.

So likewise shall my heavenly Father do also unto you, if ye from your hearts forgive not every one his brother their trespasses.

Matthew 18:28-35

This entire story was given as Jesus' answer to Peter's question in verse 21, when he asked, "Lord, how often shall I forgive my brother?"

Jesus told him this parable and ended it by saying, "So likewise shall your heavenly Father do this to you." What? "Turn you over to the tormentor because you are not forgiving your brother."

This is an excellent example of how important it is for us to forgive others.

DON'T HOLD ON TO UNFORGIVENESS!

Let me make this point plain to you right now:

If you as a black man are not forgiving the white man, or if you as a white man are not forgiving the black man, then you are putting yourselves over into the hands of the tormentor.

By not seeing that man as your brother in Christ before you saw him as a man of color, you are separating yourself from members of the Body of Christ. You are choosing to keep the Body split into factions. This only allows the devil more opportunity for divisiveness.

In this parable that Jesus gave to His disciples, the first debt owed to the king by his servant was ten thousand talents; the second debt owed to that servant by another servant was a hundred pence.

One pence equals about seventeen cents, so a hundred pence equals about seventeen dollars. In today's economy, 10,000 talents of silver is approximately $10 million, and 10,000 talents of gold is almost $20 million.

When God forgave us of our debt — our trespasses and sins — it was like forgiving us of a $20-million debt. When He asks us to forgive one another, it is like forgiving one another of a $17 debt. So likewise, if we do not forgive, we shall be turned over to the tormentor.

I said to the Lord one time: "Satan really majors on taking what appears like little technicalities and destroying us with them."

If we in the Body of Christ don't get our act together, we will find that we aren't making any progress. We will be turned over to the tormentor if we, from our hearts, will not forgive our brothers and sisters in the Lord.

It is time for us in the Body of Christ to operate in the power of agreement and unity. We *must* cancel our debts against one another.

It is time for us to be sensitive to this spirit of division. It is time for us to come together within the Body, regardless of skin color. We are one family in the Lord.

It is time for us to quit judging and condemning a person for the rest of his life because of the sins he has committed. We have an Advocate with the Father, the Lord Jesus Christ, and He can take care of our sins. He forgives us and wipes our slate clean.

The problem comes when people keep on sinning, with no fear of God. So, stop! The blood of Jesus can handle that sin, but God can't do anything for you if you have made up your mind to keep doing what you want to do for as long as you want to do it.

So, if you are in need of repentance, if you are in need of cleansing, the blood of Jesus is available, and He can wash your sins away.

Let's agree with God right now.

Heavenly Father, in the name of Jesus, according to Your Word, where there are two or three agreeing together in oneness, then anything we ask according to Your Word shall be done.

Now, in Jesus' name, forgive us, Father, for this sin of the flesh. We let go of the spirits of strife, envy, jealousy, backbiting and gossiping. We set ourselves to agree with Your Word. We want to harmonize with You by having all of our available instruments — spirit, soul and body — in line with Your Word. Cleanse us afresh and anew.

When we agree with Your Word, Father, and then with one another, we believe that we have it. We thank You, Lord, that it shall be done, in Jesus' name. Amen.

Now, rejoice and be exceedingly glad, for the Lord is good and worthy to be praised!

CHAPTER 16

ONENESS BRINGS INCREASE

I want us to look now at several passages of Scripture. We will begin with a verse from Luke's gospel, where Jesus said:

If ye have not been faithful in that which is another man's, who shall give you that which is your own?

Luke 16:12

What is going on here? Agreement.

The world wants to suck us in and have us think we don't need anybody else. But contrary to popular opinion, we do.

A question often asked in seminaries is, Am I my brother's keeper?

I will tell you this: whether or not you are your brother's keeper, you still need his agreement with whatever you are trying to do.

God's best would be for us to learn how to take our attention off ourselves and to put it on somebody else. The force that He has invested in me works better when I will turn and minister to others. What is the quickest way for us to get our prayers answered? By praying for somebody else.

AGREEMENT, IN THE BEGINNING

I used to wonder, "God, when You created Adam in the Garden, why didn't You just leave him by himself?"

The Bible says when God put Adam in the Garden, He gave him dominion and authority over the earth. Adam was given the job of naming all the living creatures, and he did. Then God looked at him and saw that it was good — except for one thing: man had no help meet, no partner. (Genesis 1:26-28; 2:18-20.)

The entire creation was based on agreement.

All the other creatures on earth were male and female, except for man. So God caused a deep sleep to come on Adam; then He took a rib from Adam's side and created Woman, who later was named Eve. (Genesis 2:21-24; 3:20.)

Let's look at the Scripture that shows Adam's response when God brought the woman to him:

And Adam said, This is now bone of my bones, and flesh of my flesh: she shall be called Woman, because she was taken out of Man.

Therefore shall a man leave his father and his mother, and shall cleave unto his wife: and they shall be one flesh.

Genesis 2:23,24

Notice how the family was made to work. A man leaves his father and his mother, and he cleaves unto his wife; then they two shall be one flesh. When they cleave together, they are to stick like glue.

How can oneness be established?

Through the power of agreement.

As previously defined in this study, to agree means to be in accord, to be in harmony, to be of one mind. It means to live in concord or without contention. Whoever said that just because you are married, you must have contention? Being in agreement is like being in symphony, when all available instruments — spirit, soul and body — are in harmony.

THEN COMES TEMPTATION

Look now in Genesis, chapter 3:

Now the serpent was more subtil than any beast of the field which the Lord God had made. And he said unto the woman, Yea, hath God said, Ye shall not eat of every tree of the garden?

Genesis 3:1

This serpent was used by Satan as a way to tempt mankind. Have you ever asked yourself why Satan didn't confront the man instead of the woman? I will tell you why: because the devil knows a woman has strong influence. The influence of a woman is a powerful thing. When used in the right way, it can produce great miracles; but when used in the wrong way, it can be wicked.

And the woman said unto the serpent, We may eat of the fruit of the trees of the garden:

But of the fruit of the tree which is in the midst of the garden, God hath said, Ye shall not eat of it, neither shall ye touch it, lest ye die.

Genesis 3:2,3

The woman already knew what had been said by God; she just had to describe it in detail.

And the serpent said unto the woman, Ye shall not surely die:

For God doth know that in the day ye eat thereof, then your eyes shall be opened, and ye shall be as gods, knowing good and evil.

Genesis 3:4,5

Doesn't this contradict what God said? Based on what Eve said in verse 3, it seems to me that God and Adam and Eve were all in agreement.

So, Satan wonders: "What can I say? What can I do? What can I present to break the agreement? As long as they are in agreement, I have no power. I can't even get into the system unless I can break their agreement. It will have to be something attractive, something they will want to do." It's as if he was saying, "Unless I can knock the lock off the door, I can't even get in the house."

The Serpent gives his argument in verse 5 by appealing to the flesh:

For God doth know that in the day ye eat thereof, then your eyes shall be opened, and ye shall be as gods, knowing good and evil.

Genesis 3:5

Breaking the power of agreement will always be directed at the lust of the flesh, the lust of the eyes and the pride of life. (1 John 2:16.) By lust, it means an intense appetite for things in the flesh, for things you can see. As for the pride of life, you might feel you have to do something to prove that another person is wrong.

And when the woman saw that the tree was good for food, and that it was pleasant to the eyes, and a tree to be desired to make one wise, she took of the fruit thereof, and did eat....

Genesis 3:6

What was it that really got the woman's attention? The Serpent's promise that the fruit would give her more ability. That caused her to break their agreement with God.

That would be another definition for sin. Every time you break an agreement with God, you are entering into sin. In the Bible, sin is called "transgression." You are actually breaking up your symphony, or harmony, with God.

Now notice that Adam was standing right there when Eve took of the fruit. The Scripture says:

...she took of the fruit thereof, and did eat, and gave also unto her husband with her; and he did eat.

Genesis 3:6

What was Satan doing through Eve? Attacking the agreement she and the man had made with God. I want you to realize that they had been walking in harmony. But then the woman was beguiled; she saw something, and she desired it. She already had everything she needed, but she was tempted to have something more.

Why didn't Adam recognize that attack against their power of agreement? He was standing right there. He could have stopped it. He could have said firmly, "We will not break our agreement." But he didn't say anything. He just gave in and, with his eyes wide open, took of the fruit that God had forbidden. So we can't blame the woman for what happened then.

Now notice what took place as a result:

> *And the eyes of them both were opened, and they knew that they were naked; and they sewed fig leaves together, and made themselves aprons.*
>
> Genesis 3:7

ONENESS — GOD'S PLAN FOR OUR LIVES

The main thing I want you to see from this story is how the spirit of oneness, the spirit of agreement, was broken between God and man.

Think about it for just a moment: What could have happened if their agreement had never been broken? The devil's business would have been closed down right then!

Would you like to know how to shut down the devil's business in your life? Quit agreeing with him, and start agreeing with God.

You are the determining witness, the establishing witness. Whichever direction your agreement goes will determine whose laws will be able to operate in the earth. If you agree with Satan by agreeing with the law of sin and death, then he can keep producing in this world. If you will agree with God by agreeing with the law of life in Christ Jesus, that means God can start producing His fruit in your life.

So, who are you agreeing with? That is the question you have to answer. Are you agreeing with the natural circumstances that are operating in your life right now, or are you agreeing with the Word of God?

Jesus said, **If ye abide in me, and my words abide in you, ye shall ask what ye will, and it shall be done unto you** (John 15:7). Wherever you add your agreement, that is where the power will be released to work in your life.

The devil won't continue coming after you and assaulting you if he finds that what he threw at you to destroy you is now being used to perfect you.

You might wonder how you can do that.

When an attack comes from the devil that was meant to destroy you, instead of agreeing with his attack, you should agree with God's Word. Then instead of being weakened, you will be strengthened. This whole thing is a matter of agreement.

When a hard time comes your way, either you can let that hard time weaken you and set you back, or you can let it move you to seek God by spending time in His Word, by praying, by fasting.

Once you decide to stay in agreement with God's plan, rather than agreeing with the plan of the devil, you will be on your way toward victory. As Scripture says, no weapon formed against you shall prosper. (Isaiah 54:17.) Again, it is all a matter of agreement.

That is the powerful thing about you and me as believers: we have been given the power to agree, and that agreement — that spirit of oneness — will produce on our behalf.

In John 17:22 Jesus, speaking to His Father about believers, says:

The glory which thou gavest me I have given them; that they may be one, even as we are one.

So, oneness is the plan of God for our lives.

But a question is asked in Amos 3:3, **Can two walk together, except they be agreed?** This provokes some thought.

SATAN'S KEY WEAPON: DIVISION

Agreement is so powerful. It will affect things in this natural, earthly realm. It will affect things in the heavenlies. And it will even affect things in the kingdom of darkness, which is the devil's territory.

I want to look in Mark's gospel, chapter 3, where Jesus asks an interesting question of His disciples:

And he called them unto him, and said unto them in parables, How can Satan cast out Satan?

And if a kingdom be divided against itself, that kingdom cannot stand.

Mark 3:23,24

This confirms the Scripture in the epistle of James, which says, **A double minded man is unstable in all his ways** (James 1:8). This man won't receive anything from the Lord. What is stopping him from receiving? The fact that he makes no decision to agree.

Jesus continues:

And if a house be divided against itself, that house cannot stand.

And if Satan rise up against himself, and be divided, he cannot stand, but hath an end.

No man can enter into a strong man's house, and spoil his goods, except he will first bind the strong man; and then he will spoil his house.

Mark 3:25-27

Let's say you are the devil and are asking yourself: *How can I cause the fall of the Church? What can I do to break up every Christian household and every Christian organization? What can I do to work against everything that harmonizes and brings humans together?*

If you, as the devil, have just read this Scripture from Mark's gospel, you will discover how you can cause the fall of man. Jesus just stated it here: "A house divided against itself cannot stand." So, you say with excitement, "I know — I'll affect man's agreement!"

As Mark 3:26 says, "If Satan be divided, he cannot stand." That means if we will divide our agreement from Satan's agreement, then he won't be able to stand in our lives. But as long as we agree with him in some way, we are allowing him the right to go ahead and bring certain things to pass in our lives.

I want you to realize this important fact: Division is the key weapon Satan will use to break our agreement in the Body of Christ.

Division!

DIVISION!!

So, we understand that the main device of the devil is division, and we understand the elements of division, which are strife, confusion and envy.

Now we have to ask ourselves, *What is it that Satan is trying to stop within the Body of Christ?*

The answer: increase.

GOD'S COVENANT BLESSING

You know, the one subject people in the Church seem to disagree about more than any other is money. I have actually had people leave my church because of my teaching on tithing.

Let me show you something now. Deuteronomy 8:18 says:

But thou shalt remember the Lord thy God: for it is he that giveth thee power to get wealth, that he may establish his covenant which he sware unto thy fathers, as it is this day.

What is this saying? It says God gives us power to get wealth so that He can do *what?* Establish His covenant, which He swore to our fathers.

God is in a position here where He has to bring His covenant to pass. Why? Because He swore it. He cannot break His Word. If He breaks His Word, then everything will be destroyed and be thrown into oblivion.

So, God has to bring this covenant to pass. What covenant? The one we find in Genesis, chapter 12:

Now the Lord had said unto Abram, Get thee out of thy country, and from thy kindred, and from thy father's house, unto a land that I will shew thee.

Genesis 12:1

God is saying to His people: "Leave your land and come to My land. Leave your system and come to My system. Leave your way and come to My way. Leave your family and come to Me."

Here is the covenant we saw being referred to in Deuteronomy 8:18:

And I will make of thee a great nation, and I will bless thee, and make thy name great; and thou shalt be a blessing:

And I will bless them that bless thee, and curse him that curseth thee: and in thee shall all families of the earth be blessed.

Genesis 12:2,3

Now notice the words spoken about God's blessing to His people in Psalm 115:

O Israel, trust thou in the Lord: he is their help and their shield.

O house of Aaron, trust in the Lord: he is their help and their shield.

Ye that fear the Lord, trust in the Lord: he is their help and their shield.

Psalm 115:9-11

Can you plainly see that you have to agree with God? You don't have any trust unless you can agree with Him and with His people.

The Lord hath been mindful of us: he will bless us; he will bless the house of Israel; he will bless the house of Aaron.

He will bless them that fear the Lord, both small and great.

The Lord shall increase you more and more, you and your children.

Psalm 115:12-14

This describes the covenant God made with Abraham, and the blessings of that covenant which will be to his descendants.

DIVISION WILL STOP INCREASE

Let's look in First Corinthians, chapter 3:

For ye are yet carnal: for whereas there is among you envying, and strife, and divisions, are ye not carnal, and walk as men?

For while one saith, I am of Paul; and another, I am of Apollos; are ye not carnal?

Who then is Paul, and who is Apollos, but ministers by whom ye believed, even as the Lord gave to every man?

I have planted, Apollos watered; but God gave the increase.

So then neither is he that planteth any thing, neither he that watereth; but God that giveth the increase.

1 Corinthians 3:3-7

This Scripture is talking about increase, about how God swore unto our fathers to bring it to pass. God was saying to Abram, "I am going to bless you and increase you with an abundant increase of favors." Psalm 115:14 says, **The Lord shall increase you more and more, you and your children.**

ENVY AND STRIFE CAUSE DIVISION

Look again at First Corinthians 3, verse 3:

For ye are yet carnal: for whereas there is among you envying, and strife, and divisions, are ye not carnal, and walk as men?

It says, **For ye are yet carnal** (or fleshly)**: for whereas there is among you envying** (or ill will)**, and strife, and divisions.** When somebody gets a promotion, instead of rejoicing with that person over it, you could become envious, or full of ill will. Then jealousy creeps in. Don't you think envy would break agreement?

We are to rejoice with those who are blessed. (Romans 12:15.) That is called agreement.

But look what is associated with envy: strife. That's the right to feel bad about that person's promotion if you want to, the right to be fussy if you want to be, the right to curse if you want to, the right to be mean if you want to be. That is strife!

What did we say agreement was? Living without contention. But notice that contention is here because strife is here.

Envy and strife produce division, don't they? Then when division is there, we know that a house divided against itself will not stand. That's what Jesus said in Mark 3:25.

SATAN WILL FIGHT TO STOP INCREASE

Now notice the apostle Paul's words in this verse:

*For while one saith, I am of Paul; and another, I am of
Apollos; are ye not carnal?*

1 Corinthians 3:4

We see this so often today.

One person says, "I am a Baptist." Another says, "I am a Methodist."

Somebody says, "I am black." Somebody else says, "I am white."

One says, "I drive a Mercedes." Another says, "I drive a Volkswagen."

What do we have here? Division.

The same question Paul had asked the Corinthian church could be asked of the Body of Christ today: Are we not carnal, or fleshly?

Romans 8:7 says about carnality, **The carnal mind is enmity against God.**

Satan is working at trying to stop increase in every area of the Christian life — in marriages, in families, in friendships, on the job.

I urge you: don't fall into the devil's trap.

Don't take strife.

Don't take envy.

Don't take jealousy.

It is God Who gives you the increase. But every time you allow carnality to work in your life, it stops up your increase. It blocks the avenue from God to you, and the covenant blessings God swore to His people are unable to come into your life.

Your being mad at me will not stop *my* increase; it only stops *your* increase.

Your refusal to talk to that brother or sister in the Lord is not stopping *their* increase; it is stopping *your* increase.

Your anger and your hatred, your gossip and your jealousy, your prejudice and your racism — all these avenues of carnality are, first and foremost, hurting you.

As long as you allow such divisions to be at work in your life, your increase will be stopped.

You may go home mad and feel that you are hurting somebody, but that other person could sleep soundly, without ever knowing what has happened. All you would be doing is stopping your own increase.

JESUS TELLS US WHAT TO DO

Jesus shares in Matthew, chapter 5, what has come to be known as the Sermon on the Mount. He is trying to adjust our attitudes. He shows us how to respond to people who have treated us in a bad way. In verse 44 He says:

Love your enemies, bless them that curse you, do good to them
that hate you, and pray for them which despitefully use you,
and persecute you.

Why?

So that we can stay in agreement with God. Then the devil will not be able to stop our increase.

But what happens if pride rises up within you and you say, "I'm not going to pray for my enemy — after what he did to me!"

That kind of attitude will only cause you to break your agreement, and right then you will have stopped your increase.

Some people don't ever get the promotions they have prayed and believed God for, because they have failed to take care of strife, envy and division — the enemies of their increase. They have allowed into their lives things that have hindered their increase and have put a stop to the very things they have been believing God for.

You must realize the devil is after your increase. The biggest enemy to Satan's attack is a clean heart. If you have darkness in your life, it is because you have given Satan a legal right to be there.

DISAGREEMENT IN MARRIAGE

Let's look in First Peter, chapter 3. Peter is addressing something I want you to pay close attention to here.

Likewise, ye husbands, dwell with them according to knowledge, giving honour unto the wife, as unto the weaker vessel, and as being heirs together of the grace of life; that your prayers be not hindered.

1 Peter 3:7

Notice this verse says, **that your prayers be not hindered.** This means simply that your prayers *can* be hindered.

What will hinder your prayers?

Disagreements.

I want you to understand the importance of a husband and wife who are sincere and dedicated believers in Jesus Christ. Together, they can accomplish whatever needs may arise within their household without any problems at all — if they will refuse to allow disagreement to enter in.

I know so many couples who harbor disagreements. They just let it sit there on the burner until it comes to a boil.

You need to realize that every time you and your spouse have an argument, when the two of you sulk around the house for a couple of days without speaking to one another, you are hurting your agreement. In fact, the power of agreement between you has been broken.

DIVISION IN MARRIAGE

Now let me show you something in Second Corinthians 6:14:

Be ye not unequally yoked together with unbelievers....

Being unequally yoked can be twofold. It can mean joining with a sinner, or it can mean joining with a Christian who just doesn't believe the way you do.

You see, if you yoke yourself with somebody who doesn't believe like you, then you are allowing strife to enter in. You had better be careful, because you are headed for trouble.

It is your responsibility to find out if a person believes like you do before you join with one another. It is serious to yoke your agreement with somebody when you haven't taken the time to find out what you are joining yourself with.

That is why marriage is so important. A couple should spend lots of time in fellowship before they join together, or they will have the wrong kind of yoke — the kind that needs to be broken.

AGREEMENT IN THE BODY OF CHRIST

Be ye not unequally yoked together with unbelievers: for what fellowship hath righteousness with unrighteousness? and what communion hath light with darkness?

And what concord hath Christ with Belial? or what part hath he that believeth with an infidel?

And what agreement hath the temple of God with idols?...

2 Corinthians 6:14-16

Let's break down this passage now and answer each of the questions the apostle Paul had asked.

...for what fellowship hath righteousness with unrighteousness?

None.

...and what communion hath light with darkness?

None.

And what concord hath Christ with Belial?

None.

...or what part hath he that believeth with an infidel?

None.

And what agreement hath the temple of God with idols?

None.

Let's continue now with verse 16:

...for ye are the temple of the living God; as God hath said, I will dwell in them, and walk in them; and I will be their God, and they shall be my people.

Wherefore come out from among them, and be ye separate, saith the Lord, and touch not the unclean thing; and I will receive you,

And will be a Father unto you, and ye shall be my sons and daughters, saith the Lord Almighty.

Having therefore these promises, dearly beloved....

2 Corinthians 6:16-18; 7:1

So, Paul says, **Having therefore these promises, dearly beloved....** What are the promises he is talking about here?

What we just read in this passage: that God will dwell in us and walk in us, that He will be our God, that we will be His people, that He will be a Father to us, that we shall be His sons and daughters.

Having therefore these promises, dearly beloved, let us cleanse ourselves from all filthiness of the flesh and spirit, perfecting holiness in the fear of God.

2 Corinthians 7:1

What is God saying to the Church through the apostle Paul?

That having therefore these promises, we have to clean ourselves up.

"AGREE AS TOUCHING"

Now let's look at Matthew 18:19:

Again I say unto you, That if two of you shall agree on earth as touching any thing that they shall ask, it shall be done for them of my Father which is in heaven.

When this says we are to "agree as touching," does that mean we have to physically touch in order to agree? Of course not. But let's look in First Corinthians, chapter 7. I want to point out something here to illustrate the meaning of "agreeing as touching."

Now concerning the things whereof ye wrote unto me: It is good for a man not to touch a woman.

1 Corinthians 7:1

Now "touching" here is referring to touching in the physical sense. The apostle Paul is talking about sexual intercourse, about a man and a woman coming together physically until a oneness has been established.

In Matthew 18:19 when Jesus said two people are to "agree as touching," He means they can come together in prayer and form a oneness concerning that which they are agreeing on. This is similar to the way a husband and wife come together physically in intercourse and make one flesh.

The significance of "agreeing as touching" is that two believers must now agree to the point that oneness is established — not physically, but spiritually.

Your prayers and your agreement with another believer will bring the two of you together in the spirit realm to make one prayer and one agreement.

You can be talking on the telephone with a believer, and the two of you can "agree as touching." You do not have to be physically touching that other person in order to "agree as touching." All you must do is decide what you will agree on together. Then when the two of you join in agreement, there will be oneness.

That is what Jesus is talking about, the kind of agreement He wants established between believers — oneness.

So, it is important that believers today join together in prayer. We must be agreeing with one another for God to move in us and through us. When we agree, and our agreement is based on God's Word, Jesus will be in the midst of our agreement, our oneness.

Why is He in the midst of our agreement? So that He can bring it to pass.

But remember this: don't allow the words of your mouth to uproot what you have started. You have to work at keeping out strife and confusion and envy. You do that, and you will be able to look up one day and say, "Behold, that which we have agreed upon has come to pass, and we are seeing the increase!" Praise the Lord!

CHAPTER 17

AGREEMENT IN WORD AND ACTION

Let's look again at Matthew 18:19,20:

Again I say unto you, That if two of you shall agree....

For where two or three are gathered together in my name, there am I in the midst of them.

The word *name* in the Greek can be translated "authority."[1] Jesus is speaking here about those who are gathered together in His authority. He is saying, "Where two or three are gathered together in My authority, I will be in their midst."

WHAT IS JESUS' AUTHORITY?

The Word is His authority. The name of Jesus is like the power of attorney (the right to use that person's name). It allows the believer to operate in that authority. Let me describe to you what this means.

Anytime you talk about using the name of a person, such as when you have been given the power of attorney, then that means being

---

[1]Strong, "Greek Dictionary of the New Testament," p. 52, #3686.

given the right to use that person's authority. My wife has power of attorney to sign my name. That gives her the right to operate in my authority.

Simply put, you could say, "In the name of Jesus, according to the Word of God, I am healed." What are you doing? You are saying: "I have the right and the authority, and I have been given the power to execute the Word of God." Psalm 149:9 says the saints of God have been honored with the authority to execute judgment that is written.

The name of Jesus is the power or the endorsement, guaranteeing us that we can get what was written in the Word of God. When we say the name of Jesus, we have said it all. Do you understand that?

Maybe as a believer you have been in a near car accident; and the moment it occurred, the only word that came out of your mouth was, "Jesus!" Earlier in your life, before you knew Jesus as Lord and Savior, the only word coming out of your mouth would probably have been an expletive. Isn't it wonderful that now in hard times we can scream out, "Jesus!" When we are full of Jesus, that is just what comes out our mouth.

Again, in Matthew 18:20 He says, "For where two or three are gathered together in My authority, there am I in the midst of them." Notice He didn't say He would be "in them"; He said He would be "in the midst of them." What else is in the midst of them? Their agreement and what they have agreed upon.

I want you to see how important it is for us to agree with the Word of God, rather than with the word of the devil or the word of the news media.

But how can you agree with God's Word if you don't know it? You can't.

AGREEMENT CAUSES ONENESS

Let's review again the definition of *agreement*. It means to be in accord, in harmony, of one mind. Agreement will always establish oneness. It means to live in concord or without contention.

It is the will of God for married couples and their families to learn how to live without contention. Marriage can be wonderful and glorious when a man and woman join together in agreement with God's Word.

Let's look again at what the Word says in Second Corinthians 6:14:

Be ye not unequally yoked together with unbelievers....

There is another aspect of being unequally yoked that I want to mention. I believe being unequally yoked involves more than marriage between a person who is born again and one who is not born again. It could also include the marriage of a mature Christian with a baby Christian. This too could create some serious marital problems.

You see, you can't be unequally yoked and think you can handle the pressures that are added to your marriage by that other yoke. You will only be putting yourself in a position to develop a new yoke around your neck!

I believe it's important that a man and woman reach a fullness of time before getting married. If the fiancé doesn't have a job to support his future wife, they have not attained the fullness of time. If they have no place to stay except at Mama's house, that is not the fullness of time. Think about it. In both situations, the couple would be living out of agreement with the Word of God. They don't need to get married and be disagreeing about what God's Word says.

The basic question a Christian couple must ask themselves is: Do we agree with God, or do we agree with the devil? Sometimes they might even try to find an in-between.

But with God, there is no in-between. That's what He said to the church of Laodicea: "You must be either hot or cold. If you try to stay in between, I will spew you out of My mouth." (Revelation 3:15,16.)

So, with no in-between, it's either God or Satan, heaven or hell, Light or darkness. There is no such thing as being "kind of" saved. You are either saved or unsaved. In fact, the Bible takes everything that is "kind of" and puts it over into darkness. When you know that you know that you know, "kind of" is nowhere to be found.

AN EXAMPLE OF AGREEMENT POWER

Now, let's look at an interesting situation described in Genesis, chapter 11.

And the whole earth was of one language, and of one speech.

Genesis 11:1

Can you imagine how that must have been? I don't know what language they spoke back then. All I know is, the Bible says at that particular time and in that particular setting, **the whole earth was of one language, and of one speech.**

And it came to pass, as they journeyed from the east, that they found a plain in the land of Shinar; and they dwelt there.

And they said one to another, Go to, let us make brick, and burn them throughly. And they had brick for stone, and slime had they for morter.

And they said, Go to, let us build us a city and a tower, whose top may reach unto heaven; and let us make us a name, lest we be scattered abroad upon the face of the whole earth.

Genesis 11:2-4

Have you ever wondered why God didn't just leave these people alone? Verse 4 gives us their objective. They were saying: "Let's establish ourselves here, lest we be scattered upon the earth."

But God wanted them scattered, because He was planning to do some things in the future. So God was forced to come into this situation.

Obviously, the people had begun their structure. Verse 5 says:

And the Lord came down to see the city and the tower, which the children of men builded.

Notice these people were not called "children of God," but "children of men."

And the Lord said, Behold, the people is one, and they have all one language; and this they begin to do: and now nothing will be restrained from them, which they have imagined to do.

Genesis 11:6

Let's look at this verse, one portion at a time.

The Lord said, Behold, the people is one. What was God saying? That the people were in agreement, that they were as one.

They have all one language. That meant all of their languages were in agreement.

And this they begin to do: and now.... I want to stop here momentarily. Notice God used the two words, **and now**. What did He mean by this? That now they were in agreement.

"THIS IS ONLY THE BEGINNING"

Let's see what this passage says in *The Amplified Bible*:

And the Lord came down to see the city and the tower which the sons of men had built.

And the Lord said, Behold, they are one people and they have
all one language; and this is only the beginning of what they
will do, and now nothing they have imagined they can do will
be impossible for them.

Genesis 11:5,6 AMP

I believe God wants us to begin to agree the way these people did in the Old Testament.

Then when we get the results of agreement, we can say, "This is only the beginning."

What are we saying then?

"I have something that is sure, something that will work every time. This is just the beginning."

Really, we would be speaking to the devil and saying: "Devil, you haven't seen anything yet! You think this is something — just wait until my spouse and I have our children agreeing with us. Just wait until our young ones start agreeing with one another. Together in our family, we will live by the power of agreement."

"NOTHING WILL BE RESTRAINED FROM THEM"

Again, Genesis 11:6 KJV says:

...and now nothing will be restrained from them, which they
have imagined to do.

I wonder how many people today have ever been lying in their bed at night and imagining how they could have certain things in their lives.

Maybe you have dreamed about owning your own business, or being out of debt, or being able to write a check for that new car, or having a house built and paying it off in only two or three payments.

We ooh and aah over such dreams, because we have not yet reached the time when we don't have to imagine it any longer, but can actually see it come into reality. But by learning about the power of agreement and then acting on it, we will start seeing results in our lives.

Notice again what is said in verse 6:

Nothing will be restrained from them.

Think about the word *restrained*. It is saying the restraints are being taken off — nothing can be held back.

It is like the floodgate is being opened for the man who knows and understands the power of oneness.

Can you see now the importance of confession? But it is not just confessing the Word.

If you and I come into agreement in some area, the words you confess may either agree or disagree with what I am believing God for. If you are going to say something, say something that will agree with what we have already established. Don't let your words be used as a shovel to dig up what we have agreed upon. I am not just confessing to be spiritual; I am confessing to release God's power by adding my agreement with yours.

LET'S SPEAK THE SAME THING

The phrase *one language* in verse 6 can be twofold — not only that they all spoke in the same language, but that they all spoke the same thing.

I believe a church has to speak the same thing. You know, I'm convinced that the biggest sin of every church in the world is the sin of the mouth. Most churches either make it or break it based on the tongues of their people.

It is the same way in your personal life, whether in your marriage, with your family or on your job. Your tongue can create a big bonfire that destroys what God has already settled. God is just waiting for your agreement.

So, how do you join your agreement with God? Obviously, in word and action. When you are willing to do that, then God says, "Let's begin."

The problem is, so many of us set our eyes on the expected end, but we don't start out right. You may be expecting a harvest, but it will never happen if you don't ever plant the seed.

I have heard this complaint from people: "Well, Pastor, you ought not talk about money all the time. It just makes us feel uncomfortable."

That means those people are probably struggling with the love of money. Anything you can't release is what you love.

I refuse to stop talking to my congregation about tithing. I will keep teaching it and teaching it. I don't care if everybody leaves. This principle is right, and it is of God. We are supposed to tithe as an honor to our heavenly Father. That's what the Word says.

Anytime I get to the point where God tells me to give something away and I have a problem releasing it, I know then that I *must* get rid of it.

LET'S QUIT MAGNIFYING DIFFERENCES

I am not going to stop talking about racism, either. I will continue talking about it to the Body of Christ, because it's wrong. There is nothing in Scripture that says one person can dislike another person because of the color of his skin.

We cannot keep magnifying our differences. As I had mentioned earlier in this book, there are ministers today who teach that everybody in the Bible was black. But that kind of teaching only causes division within the Church.

There were all kinds of people in the Bible. There were Greeks, Hebrews, Ethiopians, as well as others. So, who do we blacks think we are? Just being black doesn't mean we can magnify a difference. That will only lead to division.

The spirit of division causes men who are strong in the Lord to go back to the same helpless place they were spiritually before they got saved. The spirit of division wants to divide the Body of Christ and cause us to fall apart by magnifying differences with the influence of hate.

I have never said there were no blacks in the Bible. Part of the Bible took place in Africa. But should we use that point to create a strong movement that only magnifies the differences? No.

The spirit of division always magnifies the differences. Then when division is there, agreement cannot be there — and the devil knows that. He will keep on magnifying differences in order to keep division alive within the Body of Christ.

WE WERE DESIGNED TO AGREE WITH GOD

Now let me show you something in Luke, chapter 5. This is a wonderful Scripture.

And he spake also a parable unto them; No man putteth a piece of a new garment upon an old; if otherwise, then both the new maketh a rent, and the piece that was taken out of the new agreeth not with the old.

And no man putteth new wine into old bottles; else the new wine will burst the bottles, and be spilled, and the bottles shall perish.

But new wine must be put into new bottles; and both are preserved.

Luke 5:36-38

Do you see the danger of trying to make certain things agree when they don't? If you take something new, something different, and try to coordinate it with things that don't agree, they will never produce. You cannot mix a horse and a cat; they were not designed to agree.

As a born-again believer, you were not designed to agree with hell and the devil. You have been designed to agree with God. But it's your choice — you can agree with the things of the devil if you want to.

The Scripture says new wine must be put in new bottles. You can't take the truths you find in the Word of God and apply them to your life if you have failed to make certain changes. God is a holy God. You can't be operating in the gifts of the Spirit if you refuse to allow the fruit of the Spirit to be produced in your life. By operating that way, your gift will only become perverted.

When I receive the Word of God, and the gifts of the Spirit are operating in my life, I want to make sure the new wine Jesus speaks of is going into a new bottle. Scripture says, **Old things are passed away; behold, all things are become new** (2 Corinthians 5:17). This new life in Jesus cannot correlate with an old way of living.

If you go to church to receive the Word of God and are being taught new things, you can't be continuing to live that old way of life at home. You can't keep shacking up with your boyfriend/girlfriend. By doing that, you are showing that you haven't really changed your life, and you would be living in hypocrisy. That kind of life will never produce any results.

You have to fix those old things at home. Then the new things you are learning in God's Word will be in agreement with the new way of life you are living at home.

You cannot take new principles and apply them to old ways of thinking. That is why the Bible talks about renewing your mind. (Romans 12:2.) What are you renewing your mind to do? To be in agreement with God's Word. This is a simple principle that, when applied to your life, will produce great and mighty things.

First, you have to believe in your heart that what God's Word says is true. Then you have to verbalize it, saying, "God, I agree with You and with Your Word." You can begin this new life and see the manifestation of God's power by just agreeing.

What are you believing God for? If you can find it in God's Word, just say from your heart and with your mouth, "Lord, I agree with this, and I will express my agreement in word and in action."

WHAT HAPPENS WHEN AGREEMENT IS BROKEN?

The last portion of this pledge is where a lot of people miss it. They agree with the Word they hear at church; but when they go home, they disagree with that Word through their own words and actions. Then they wonder why they don't see the manifestation. The answer is simple: because they broke their agreement with God.

In our society, when you break an agreement, there are consequences. The same is true when you break agreement in the spiritual realm. The consequences of breaking agreement in the spirit world will be to affect the physical manifestation.

What must we do if we break agreement? Repent quickly. I will use an analogy.

Let's say we take a piece of paper, fold it down the middle and slowly rip it into two pieces. All we have to do is tear it a little bit at a time; then before long, one side will be completely separated from the other side.

That's what happens when we break our agreement with God. Just as with a slight tear down the middle of that paper, there comes a tear within us that separates us just a little bit from God.

Now we may have broken our agreement with God, but we don't have to stay that way. All we have to do is to repent immediately and say, "Lord, I'm sorry; I repent." Once we have done that, an adjustment can be made, and the gap between God and ourselves can be closed.

But do you know what happens so many times? We say, "Lord, I'm not worthy. I just feel so dirty, so nasty. I don't deserve Your forgiveness." Then that tear between God and us becomes a little deeper.

When we finally reach the point where we are willing to turn back to God, the tear within us must be mended in order to get it all back together again.

When the agreement is first broken, there is just a small crack. It is so much easier for us to repent quickly. Then we can close that gap by getting back into agreement with God.

God is saying, "If you should do something that breaks the agreement, don't let condemnation rise up within you; repent quickly."

When you do that, you can get back in union and oneness with God. You will be able, then, to receive the manifestation of what you have agreed upon.

Condemnation will only dam up what you had been trying to receive from God. Don't sit there, saying, "I knew I couldn't do this in the first place; I'm not going to be a hypocrite." When you miss it, don't be condemning yourself like that; repent and get back together with God. Say, "Lord, I repent; please forgive me."

Then the process of living your life in God can continue on. Remember, though, when a piece of paper is torn apart, it has to be taped back together again. So, it may take time for some healings to occur within you. But you must be willing to allow time for that cleansing process to take place as you are washed in His blood.

God is so good to meet us on our level. He recognizes when we have made a mistake, but all we have to do is turn to Him and repent from our hearts. He is a loving Father Who is willing to forgive and to forget. Hallelujah!

I want you to think about what you have read and to release your faith now by agreeing with God and His Word. Then the Father can bring it to pass.

Lift your hands and agree with God concerning your situation.

If you are sick, God has already said in His Word that you are healed. Say, "Father, I agree that You have established healing for my body. I receive it, in Jesus' name."

If you have financial problems, say: "Father, I agree with Your Word that says You will meet my needs according to Your riches in glory by Christ Jesus. I agree with that, and thank You for it."

I want you to start experiencing agreement right now. Lift your heart to God and agree with Him in whatever area you need agreement. Open your mouth and release it to Him. Agree with Him by faith for it to come to pass, in Jesus' name. Your God is a loving and merciful God. He will meet you right where you are.

CONCLUSION

I started off several years ago thinking God wanted me to teach on the topic of "Understanding God's Purpose for the Anointing." Then He spoke to my heart and said, "There can be no move of the anointing as long as there is division and separation and racism within My Body."

I don't want to be responsible for stopping the glory of God from coming to my house because I operated in the spirit of division and separation. No matter what it takes for the Body of Christ to get out of this bondage, I have been willing to speak the truth.

People told me I was crazy to do it. They said: "Don't try it; it will only get you into trouble. If you preach this message, Brother Dollar, people will hate you for it, and your ministry will be destroyed." Well, I have been willing to take my chances.

Maybe you are sick right now because you have been harboring this spirit of racism in your heart. But I want you to know you can be set free of it. It takes faith to do it; but if you will step out by faith, in Jesus' name, your miracle is at hand.

Throughout the years, maybe your heart has been hardened. Now it is time for you to break free of that hardened heart. In the name of Jesus, I invite the spirit of reconciliation to rise up within you.

Let's show the world that the Church knows how to handle this spirit of division, separation and racism.

Are you a black person who has had feelings in your heart against white people?

Are you a white person who has had feelings in your heart against black people?

Are you a Mexican or Hispanic person who has had feelings in your heart against either the blacks or the whites?

It is important for you to realize that the spirit of division has affected the Body of Christ long enough. It's time that this spirit of division be broken within the Church.

I pray you are willing now to take the necessary steps that will bring healing and restoration to the Body. Your willingness to do this will start a move of God that cannot be stopped.

If you are white, I want you to go to a black person. I want you to look that person square in the eyes, then I want you to repent and to apologize for the sins of your ancestors against black people. Be willing to say from your heart, "I am sorry."

If you are black, I want you to go to a white person. I want you to look that person square in the eyes, then I want you to repent for the years of unforgiveness towards white people that you have carried in your heart.

If you, as a believer, have had feelings of hate, distrust or hostility towards people of any other race, it's vitally important that you go to some member of that race and repent of those feelings. Look that person square in the eyes and say this from your heart:

> I am asking You, in Jesus' name, to forgive me for the feelings I have had in the past against your race. I am sorry for the sin I have held down deep in my heart. It was wrong, and

I repent of it now. I will give no more place to that spirit of division and that spirit of separation, in Jesus' name.

I need you; you need me; we need one another. So let's hook arms together and walk forward in the love God has shown to each of us through the shed blood of His Son, Jesus Christ.

Your heart may be filled with fear at the idea of doing this. You may be thinking, *I just don't know if I can do it.*

Let me remind you of the blood Jesus shed for you. Don't worry about how you feel; do this in honor of His blood. There may be people you don't want to forgive, but it's because of the blood of Jesus that God has forgiven you. So, remember that.

Why not join with me in prayer? Let's open our hearts to God as we pray for true reconciliation within the Body of Christ. This spirit of reconciliation will change your life, it will change your family, it will change your church. It can even spread throughout your city, changing the hearts of all those people who are willing to repent.

Father, in the name of Jesus, I pray You will make real in our hearts the great importance of the ministry of reconciliation. I pray we will arm ourselves with Your Word and stand against this devilish spirit of division and separation that has risen in this earth. I pray, Lord, that our Church, the Body of Christ, will welcome all races without magnifying their differences.

I thank You for the blood of Jesus that was poured out for us, so that we could be reconciled and restored back into union with You. In honor of that blood, we now repent of any anger; of any unforgiveness; of any feelings that have separated us from family members, from friends, from other members of the Body of Christ; of anything that would keep us from praying for our enemies.

I now move in the ministry of reconciliation to declare before You, by faith, that these walls of division within the Body of Christ have fallen. I bind the spirit of division and separation from coming back into our lives. I pray that the spirit of prejudice shall not enter again in any area of our lives. We have been given the word of reconciliation, and we have been anointed to carry it out.

Right now by faith, Father, we walk in this ministry of reconciliation. I pray that our broken marriages be reconciled, that these husbands and wives be reconciled in honor of Your blood. I pray for employers and employees where problems exist between them, that they be reconciled in honor of Your blood.

It doesn't matter who was right or who was wrong in any area; we are anointed to operate in the ministry of reconciliation, and that ministry of reconciliation will change the hardest heart. If You can change the priests and cause them to be obedient to the faith, You can change even our enemies. So, Lord, we receive that ministry of reconciliation right now.

Give us more and more revelation on reconciliation as we live in it, as we walk in it, as we move in it day by day. May we no longer look at one another and judge one another by our flesh. We will no longer take into account one another's past. In honor of Jesus' blood, I pray that we be reconciled. Thank You for it, Lord.

Because of our decision to walk in the ministry of reconciliation, I pray that Your anointing to heal broken hearts is rising up all across this country. We give You praise and honor for it, Lord. In Jesus' name. Amen.

Creflo A. Dollar Jr. is pastor and founder of World Changers Ministries Christian Center, a non-denominational church located in College Park, Georgia.

Formerly an educational therapist, Creflo Dollar began the ministry in 1986 with eight people. He is now an international teacher and conference speaker with a congregation of over 17,000.

Creflo Dollar has been called of God to teach the Gospel with simplicity and understanding. He can be seen and heard throughout the world on "Changing Your World" broadcasts via television and radio.

For a brochure of books and tapes
by Creflo A. Dollar, Jr., write:

World Changers Ministries
P. O. Box 490124
College Park, GA 30349

*Please include your prayer requests and comments
when you write.*

Other Books by Creflo A. Dollar Jr.

Answers Awaiting in the Presence of God

Uprooting the Spirit of Fear

Available from your local bookstore.

HARRISON HOUSE
Tulsa, Oklahoma 74153

For copies of this book
in Canada, contact:

Word Alive
P. O. Box 670
Niverville, Manitoba
CANADA R0A 1E0

The Harrison House Vision

Proclaiming the truth and the power
Of the Gospel of Jesus Christ
With excellence;

Challenging Christians to
Live victoriously,
Grow spiritually,
Know God intimately.